Liturgy and Ministry in Times of Need

Wendy Cichanski Caduff

Ann Dickinson Degenhard

Bernard Evans

Anne Y. Koester

LITURGY
TRAINING
PUBLICATIONS

Nihil Obstat   *Imprimatur*
Rev. Mr. Daniel G. Welter, JD   Most Rev. Ronald A. Hicks
Chancellor   Vicar General
Archdiocese of Chicago   Archdiocese of Chicago
March 26, 2020   March 26, 2020

LITURGY AND MINISTRY IN TIMES OF NEED © 2020 Archdiocese of Chicago: Liturgy Training Publications, 3949 South Racine Avenue, Chicago, IL 60609; 800-933-1800; fax: 800-933-7094; email: orders@ltp.org; website: www. LTP.org. All rights reserved.

This book was edited by Danielle A. Noe. Michael A. Dodd was the production editor, Anna Manhart was the designer, and Luis Leal was the production artist.

Art © Nancy Marek Cote

24 23 22 21 20   1 2 3 4 5

Printed in the United States of America

Library of Congress Control Number: 2020932619

ISBN: 978-1-61671-568-7

LMTN

This book is dedicated to all those who have suffered and to those who love them—especially the victims of crimes against humanity, natural disasters, and acts of hatred and violence. May they always know the love of God, for "it bears all things, believes all things, hopes all things, [and] endures all things."

—1 Corinthians 13:7

CONTENTS

INTRODUCTION

The proclamation of the Gospel will be a basis for restoring the dignity of human life. . . . To live our human life to the fullest and to meet every challenge as a leaven of Gospel witness in every culture and in every city will make us better Christians and bear fruit in our cities.

—The Joy of the Gospel, 75

Jesus told the story of the Good Samaritan and the parable of the Last Judgment. He was moved by the suffering of people around him as he healed the sick, fed the hungry crowds, and returned sight to those who were blind. This man from Galilee told the disciples that their love of God was measured by their love of neighbor, a love shown in acts of compassion and mercy.

Jesus proclaimed the Good News that God's reign has broken through, and that we are to repent and believe. He also announced, again and again, what this news required of his followers in daily living—respond to our neighbors' needs wherever and whenever we encounter them. Our acceptance of Jesus and his saving message frees us to reach out and ease the suffering of anyone we meet, frees us to be that Samaritan on the road to Jericho. As we do this we not only live as Jesus commanded, but we proclaim his Good News. Our loving actions toward our neighbor become a witness to the Good News, a form of evangelizing. This is a core message of Christian discipleship, and it has been proclaimed throughout the ages.

St. Paul's letters carry references to collections taken up to assist Christians in other locations experiencing difficult times. The third-century bishop of Carthage, Cyprian, urged Christians to give generously to persons stricken by a plague in North Africa, and to give whether the victims were Christians or pagans.[1] Another third-century writer, Clement of Alexandria, encouraged Christians to share with persons in need and not try to distinguish too carefully between the deserving and the undeserving.[2]

---

1. *On Works and Almsgiving*, 5, 17, 24; Ante-Nicene Fathers, vol. 5. Peabody, MA: Hendrickson Publishers, 1999.
2. *Who Is the Rich Man That Shall Be Saved?*, 33; Ante-Nicene Fathers, vol. 2. Peabody, MA: Hendrickson Publishers, 1999.

In modern times, Pope Benedict XVI reminds us that Jesus Christ has universalized the command to love our neighbor. Our neighbor is anyone "who needs me, and whom I can help" (*God Is Love*, 15). Responding to our neighbors' needs—whether immediate or long-term, caused by lack of resources or by some unforeseen emergency—is central to the Christian's life. It is a challenge to every faithful Christian and to every parish seeking to guide Jesus' disciples to live out his call to "repent, and believe in the gospel" (Mark 1:15).

CHARITY AND JUSTICE

Christians today recognize with ever greater clarity that their faith calls them to acts of charity. We are coming to appreciate as well that charitable acts are the first step in our movement toward justice. Our Church long ago recognized that participation in the transformation of the world is "a constitutive dimension of the preaching of the Gospel" (*Justice in the World*, 6). It belongs to the mission of the Church.

It is likewise an expectation of every member of the Church to build communities and a society where everyone can have their needs met. As Pope Francis pointed out: "An authentic faith—which is never comfortable or completely personal—always involves a deep desire to change the world" (*The Joy of the Gospel*, 183). For us to meet this expectation we need to be clear about how acts of charity and acts of justice relate to each other.

The former represents our first response to another person's needs, immediate giving to relieve the present suffering of a fellow human. The latter, acts of justice, aim to help that person or group move from depending on others to caring for themselves and contributing to society's well-being.

Pope Benedict XVI summarized this relationship between acts of charity and those of justice when he wrote: "To love someone is to desire that person's good and to take effective steps to secure it" (*Charity in Truth*, 7). Later in this document, quoting Paul VI, he noted that "the individual who is animated by true charity labors skillfully to discover the causes of misery, to find the means to combat it, to overcome it resolutely" (*Charity in Truth*, 30). This is the work of social justice. Jesus' command to love our neighbor cannot stop short of this work to change or remove every cause of that neighbor's suffering.

LITURGY AND LIFE

In the Catholic Tradition, a major part of this guidance and formation of the Christian unfolds in our liturgical prayer. When the assembly gathers to praise and worship God, it also celebrates and gives thanks for who we are—a people loved, redeemed, and empowered to change our lives and the world around us. We celebrate the fact that through Jesus Christ our relationships with our God and with our sisters and brothers have been restored.

At the same time we recognize our responsibility to go forth from the liturgy—especially our Eucharistic celebration—and work to change anything in our lives and in society that contradicts this Good News of restored relationships. We must, in other words, address such issues as immigration, racism, poverty, homelessness, and lack of healthcare in whatever way is possible for our state in life.

This link between liturgy and justice has been part of the Judeo-Christian reality from the beginning. The prophets of the Old Testament repeatedly warned that worship which does not lead to acts of justice is mere ritual with little value.

> With what shall I come before the LORD,
> and bow before God most high?
> Shall I come before him with burnt offerings,
> with calves a year old?
>
> Will the LORD be pleased with thousands of rams,
> with myriad streams of oil?
> Shall I give my firstborn for my crime,
> the fruit of my body for the sin of my soul?
>
> You have been told, O mortal, what is good,
> and what the LORD requires of you:
> Only to do justice and to love goodness,
> and to walk humbly with your God.
>
> —Micah 6:6–8

"To do justice" in the prophetic literature carries very practical implications as we see in Isaiah, Jeremiah, and Amos: let the oppressed go free, share your bread with the hungry, bring the homeless poor into your house, visit those who are in prison, care for those who are sick, and treat the immigrant as one of your own.

In modern times, this understanding of liturgy moving us to acts of justice is present in various teaching documents of the Catholic Church. One example, again from Pope Benedict XVI, is the encyclical *God Is Love*.

The Holy Father reminds Catholics that worship, especially Eucharistic communion "includes the reality of being loved and of loving others in turn. A Eucharist which does not pass over into the concrete practice of love is intrinsically fragmented" (*God Is Love,* 14). He added that "love for widows and orphans, prisoners, and the sick and needy of every kind, is as essential to her [the Church] as the ministry of the sacraments and the preaching of the Gospel" (*God Is Love,* 22).

Our communal worship—our liturgy—must lead us to enter ever more fully into the ministry of charity and justice in the world. Therein lies a challenge for pastoral leadership in every congregation. How might our liturgical celebrations become the experience that forms those present to continue living the Eucharist as they leave the assembly and to remember that the faith we proclaim in ritual is real only if it is lived in the streets?

The chance of that happening increases when our liturgies reflect what is happening in that world, in our society, in our daily lives. The homily, Universal Prayer (or Prayer of the Faithful), and the selection of music can support this effort. Every act of the liturgy has the potential to connect our worship with our lived experiences. Our public worship must never become a "time-out" moment where we seek to escape the griefs and sorrows, the conflicts and tensions, the suffering and injustices that mark our life in society. Liturgy must acknowledge these realities and fill us with "a deep desire to change the world."[3]

It is not only the liturgy that must connect us to real life and real needs in our community, society, and world. This is the task also of every parish ministry: catechesis, outreach, sacramental preparation, adult faith formation, liturgical training sessions, and so on. The more parish ministries make this connection, the more parishioners will appreciate that their liturgical prayer, their faith, their religion is about their life in the world. If this happens on a daily basis in the life of a parish, it will not be difficult for the pastoral leadership to engage the faithful in responding to crises and emergencies happening anywhere.

We should note as well that for the local Church to encourage Catholics to engage in social, economic, and political matters of society is not politicizing the religious mission of the Church. It is, rather, a simple recognition that we humans are social beings shaped and influenced by happenings in every area of our lives. It is a recognition that living conditions can affect how well we do or do not grow as morally responsible persons, how well we do or do not respond to God's saving grace. In the words of the Second Vatican Council, "But this sense of responsibility will not be achieved unless

---

3.   Pope Francis, homily at the Church of the Gesu in Rome; January 3, 2014.

people are so circumstanced that they are aware of their dignity and are capable of responding to their calling in the service of God and humanity" (*Pastoral Constitution on the Church in the Modern World*, 31).

This is a religious concern, and it belongs to the mission of every parish. Proclaiming the Good News of Jesus Christ—evangelizing—must take into account how the Gospel intersects with peoples' lives. As Pope Francis stated: "An evangelizing community gets involved by word and deed in people's daily lives" (*The Joy of the Gospel*, 24).

HOW TO USE THIS BOOK

This book is a practical resource to assist local churches in guiding parishioners to respond to persons in need. More specifically, it is a pastoral resource on liturgy and outreach in times of emergency and crisis. Organized by particular need, this book will help parish staff in discerning how to respond to such tragedies as mass shootings, natural and environmental disasters, pandemics, sudden deaths, accidents, or predicaments affecting the local community, and situations affecting human dignity, such as immigrant children being separated from parents at the United States and Mexican border.

As a parish resource, this book provides ideas and practical guidance for pastoral ministers on catechizing and forming the assembly in relation to a particular crisis that develops. It will help parish staff explain why parishioners should care about the situation. What does this have to do with our faith? How is it the business of our parish? Why should I see my response as a way of living out Jesus' command to love my neighbor? How can I view our response as a way of responding to Jesus' proclamation that the reign of God is upon us?

It is always the mission of a parish to form its members in the love that Jesus showed towards persons who were blind, lame, outcast, lonely, sick, or carrying any kind of need. That is a given, not only for a social ministry committee within the parish, but for all the parish ministries—especially those relating to liturgy and catechesis.

Today, however, there is a growing urgency for parishes to respond to crises and emergencies. Mass shootings occur in the United States at an ever-increasing rate. Weather events are more frequent and more severe

> Christ has no body now on earth but yours; no hands but yours; no feet but yours. Yours are the eyes through which the compassion of Christ must look out on the world. Yours are the feet with which he is to go about doing good. Yours are the hands with which he is to bless his people.
>
> —St. Teresa of Avila

than at any time in our memory. Forest fires ravage draught-stricken lands threatening human lives and all other living creatures. Our nation's broken immigration policies result in families being traumatized by deportation raids. Our global community struggles with economic rebuilding after COVID-19.

These are twenty-first-century realities that our local churches cannot ignore. Most Christians are willing, even eager, to help out when others face such crises. What is sometimes lacking is a parish's ability to guide members in responding from a faith perspective. Too often parish staff struggle to find an appropriate and creative way to connect the various ministries with an emergency whether local or distant. It is the purpose of this book to assist parish staff in this task.

—Bernard Evans

ABOUT THE AUTHORS

Wendy Cichanski Caduff, MA, shares both family life and professional ministry with her husband, Ben. She is the mother of two young children, having come to motherhood through the gift of open adoption. She is a lay ecclesial minister, coordinating the Caring Ministries office at the Basilica of St. Mary in Minneapolis. Prior to this, she served as pastoral associate, director of faith formation, and a Catholic school teacher at various parishes in dioceses around Minnesota. She is formed by the social teachings of the Church, empowered by feminist theology, and feels both the urgency and the primacy of conversations surrounding race and the environment. She holds a master of arts in pastoral ministry from St. John's University in Collegeville, Minnesota. She has been contributor to *Give Us This Day* published by Liturgical Press since its inception and enjoys writing about the sacred through the lens of the ordinary, everyday stuff of life. This is her first book. Wendy is the primary writer of the ministerial outreach components.

Ann Dickinson Degenhard, MDiv, earned her degree from St. John's School of Theology in Collegeville, Minnesota, and her bachelor of arts from St. Norbert College in De Pere, Wisconsin. Having served as a hospital chaplain and teacher, Ann has spent her recent years writing catechetical resources and raising her two children. She has written for past editions of *Sourcebook for Sundays, Seasons, and Weekdays; Children's Liturgy of the Word; Celebrating the Lectionary®; Sunday Prayer for Teens;* and *The Living Word™.* Ann lives in rural Illinois and enjoys reading and martial arts. Ann contributed to the ministerial outreach sections.

Bernard Evans, PHD, is retired faculty at St. John's University, Collegeville, Minnesota, where he served as associate dean for faculty in the school of theology. Evans also occupied the Virgil Michel Ecumenical Chair in Rural Social Ministries, teaching courses on Christian social ethics, environmental theology, and ministry in rural communities. His most recent publications include the books *Lazarus at the Table: Catholics and Social Justice* (2006), *Vote Catholic? Beyond the Political Din* (2008), *Stewardship: Living a Biblical Call* (2014), as well as a chapter, "Care for Creation," in *A Vision of Justice*, edited by Ron Pagnucco and Susan Crawford Sullivan (2014), all published by Liturgical Press. Bernie wrote the introduction.

Anne Y. Koester, JD, MA (theology), works at Georgetown University, Washington, DC, where she is also an adjunct instructor with the theology department. In addition, she oversees the RCIA process at Holy Trinity Catholic Church in DC. A former trial lawyer, Anne studied theology at St. John's University in Collegeville, Minnesota. She has worked at the Notre Dame Center for Pastoral Liturgy and the Georgetown Center for Liturgy. Anne is the author of *Sunday Mass: Our Role and Why It Matters* (Liturgical Press, 2007), editor of *Liturgy and Justice: To Worship God in Spirit and in Truth* (Liturgical Press, 2002), and coeditor of *Vision: The Scholarly Contributions of Mark Searle to Liturgical Renewal* (Liturgical Press, 2004) and *Called to Participate: Theological, Ritual and Social Perspectives* by Mark Searle (Liturgical Press, 2006). She is a member of the editorial advisory council of Liturgical Press and a member of the North American Academy of Liturgy. Anne wrote the liturgy and prayer sections.

CHAPTER ONE

Acts against Human Dignity

Beloved, let us love one another, because love is of God.

—1 John 4:7

THEOLOGICAL AND SOCIAL CONTEXT

I remember the image vividly. I can still see the red shirt, the blue shorts, and the brown shoes. It brought me to tears when I first saw it, and it still does each time I search for the image online. The little boy, face down, washed up on the shore, having drowned as his boat capsized in the Mediterranean. Deep sobs escape me as I imagine his plight and mourn this young life cut short, the potential unlived. His name was Alan Kurdi, and he was just three years old when he died on September 2, 2015. His five-year-old brother died that day as well. They were among sixteen people in a small boat leaving Bodrum, Turkey, in an attempt to reach Greece. Their boat, built for eight people, capsized within five minutes.

Alan was just one victim of the millions who are fleeing to safety from Syria. But, the image of his young toddler body laying lifeless went viral, and images are powerful. The world seemed to awaken and take notice of what was going on in Syria, however briefly. Too many humans in over-crowded rubber boats or dinghies setting out in the dark of night. Boats with not enough life vests. Life vests that were not actual life vests, but rather cheap imitations. Life savings being drained and paid to smugglers in a desperate attempt to reach Europe. Promises made, promises broken. Boats capsizing and families being tossed overboard into the icy waters, some were rescued but most drowned. Other boats make it to land, only to be turned away again on Europe's shores. The nightmare goes on and on for those whose homeland is being ravaged by war.

Numbers are difficult to estimate, but since the civil war in Syria began, casualties range from 370,000 to 570,000 people dead. Those still living are fleeing war and the brutal occupation of the Islamic fundamentalists in their homeland, commonly known as the Islamic State. Surrounding countries see the need and are responding in varying degrees.

When Pope Francis visited the United States Congress, he reminded those gathered:

> Our world is facing a refugee crisis of a magnitude not seen since the Second World War. This presents us with great challenges and many hard decisions. . . . We must not be taken aback by their numbers, but rather view them as persons, seeing their faces and listening to their stories, trying to respond as best we can to their situation. To respond in a way which is always humane, just, and fraternal.

This plea by Pope Francis is in line with more than a century of strong social teaching by the Church, based firmly on the notion that there is dignity in each and every person, and that the glory of God shines through us all because each of us is made in his image and likeness. This is central to the Church's commitment to the treatment of migrants and refugees, regardless of what papers are carried. St. John Paul II taught that ministering to the needs of the refugee or the migrant does not depend on legal status: "An irregular legal status cannot allow the migrant to lose his [or her] dignity, since he [or she] is endowed with inalienable rights that can neither be violated nor ignored."[1]

The glory of God is the human person fully alive.
— St. Irenaeus

Our Church is also guided by strong biblical examples and mandates. In the Old Testament, we meet a God who liberated the captives and was on the side of the oppressed in Exodus and who called on Abraham to abandon his home and migrate to a new land, and we hear how Jacob and the Israelites followed Joseph to Egypt as migrants to escape a famine in their homeland. The New Testament begins with Jesus' parents looking for shelter and depending upon the hospitality of others as Mary is about to give birth. Then, soon after his birth, they crossed borders and fled danger to escape a dangerous ruler who was slaughtering innocents (see Mathew

---

1. Message of Pope John Paul II for World Migration Day; July 25, 1995.

2:13–15). From there, we see time and time again how Jesus interacted with the outcast, lowly, and downtrodden in all of the Gospel stories and his very clear teaching in Matthew 25 titled The Judgment of the Nations.

In that parable, there is a separation of sheep and goats. I'm not sure why the sheep get the better end of the end of the deal, because goats are fine creatures as well, but they do. They are placed on the shepherd's right, and they are blessed. They are inheriting the kingdom that has been prepared since the very foundation of the world. The king in the parable looks at those on the right and says to them, "You gave me food when I was hungry, you gave me drink when I was thirsty, you clothed me when I was naked, cared for me when I was ill, visited me in prison, and welcomed me when I was a stranger" (author's paraphrase). The righteous protest, saying they did not see the king in need and do any of those things. And here's the beautiful part. The king's response is: "Amen, I say to you, whatever you did for one of the least brothers or sisters of mine, you did for me" (Matthew 25:40). The parable clearly spells out to the goats that when they did none of those things to a person in need, it is as if they did not do it for Christ himself. Thus, eternal reward or eternal punishment is the outcome. Matthew 25 has long been the yardstick of my life as a Christian because Christ could not be much clearer about what he expects of each and every one of us. I fall short with this measurement quite often, but I hold myself up to it nonetheless. I hold myself up to it, and I hold our cities, states, and nations up to it as I look around at the very real needs surrounding us.

> The Gospel requires that particular care be taken to welcome into the Church's assembly those often discarded by society—the socially and economically marginalized, the elderly, the sick, those with disabilities, and those with special needs.
>
> —*Built of Living Stones*, 42

LITURGY AND PRAYER

"A strange thing takes place in prayer," writes Michael Casey, OCSO. "There is a mysterious coupling of our own life with the lives of others—an embrace that includes the whole of humanity."[2] He adds that "from this widened prayer develops a wider compassion that finds expression in my daily life. Less and less do I see myself as distinct from the pain of others. More and more I find myself assuming part of their burdens."[3]

---

2. Michael Casey, *Toward God: The Ancient Wisdom of Western Prayer* (Ligouri, MO: Ligouri/Triumph, 1996), 19.

3. Casey, *Toward God*, 19.

Casey's words capture an essential dimension of all prayer, both personal and liturgical—it should expand our sense of oneness with all humanity. Christians do not lead isolated lives; rather, we see ourselves as intimately bound up in a web of relationships. God shares life with all human persons; created in God's image and likeness, every human life is sacred and, as such, every person possesses a fundamental dignity. As people formed through our prayer, then, any act that threatens to deprive even one person of this dignity and deny the sense of the sacred that is within him or her startles us, moves us to tears and outrage, and compels us to protect and care for the person who is mistreated. We are much too interrelated to be unconcerned about these profound injustices.

> From the liturgy, therefore, particularly the eucharist, grace is poured forth upon us as from a fountain; the liturgy is the source for achieving in the most effective way possible human sanctification and God's glorification, the end to which all the Church's other activities are directed.
>
> —Constitution on the Sacred Liturgy, 10

When we gather for liturgy in the face of acts against human dignity, we need, in the words of Mark Searle, "to hear what we are saying when we pray, reflect on what we do when we celebrate." He goes on to say that the liturgy will not allow us "to lose sight of who we are and what we are called to. It will not allow us to forget."[4] We can complete his sentence in light of present circumstances in our own communities. For instance, liturgy, and by extension communal prayer that is alongside liturgy, will not allow us to forget children and families who are fleeing violence and who suffer and even die in their desperation to find a safe place to live. It will not allow us to forget the millions of people who fall into the hands of traffickers and are sold into slavery. It will not allow us to forget our sisters and brothers who suffer because of racist taunts and assaults on their person. It will not allow us to forget the people of faith who suffer discrimination because of their religious beliefs and practices. It will not allow us to forget that often these injustices are intertwined.

IMMEDIATE RESPONSE

Soon after a crisis occurs, parishes need to be prepared to call people to gather for prayer in response to a wide variety of injustices. Communities will be impacted in different ways because the injustices that are most visible in one community might be less so (although likely not nonexistent) in others. A simple framework for a prayer service (such as Evening Prayer)

---

4. Mark Searle, "Grant Us Peace . . . Do We Hear What We Are Saying?," a talk (date unknown) published in Stephen Wilbricht, *Rehearsing God's Just Kingdom: The Eucharistic Vision of Mark Searle* (Collegeville, MN: Liturgical Press, 2013), 225.

Liturgy and Ministry in Times of Need

will allow parishes to adapt it to speak to the particular community's experiences and needs and to do so as often as necessary.[5]

When preparing prayer services in response to this crisis, you will need to consider who will be present. Are there parishioners and others in the local community who are refugees, asylum applicants, recent migrants or immigrants? How might they be invited to participate in the parish's worship? It will also be important to consider the language groups present to ensure the songs, readings, and prayers are accessible to all. If the prayer is in response to racism or religious discrimination, how can the parish reach out to those whose dignity has been attacked? Has anyone died as the result of an act against human dignity? How will these individuals be remembered? In these circumstances, the names of the deceased can be inscribed in the parish's *Book of the Names of the Dead.*

For the liturgical environment, simplicity will be meaningful and have broad appeal. A cross or crucifix, an icon of Christ—for example, the Good Shepherd, the Savior, the Life-Giver would be fitting—along with candles for an opening candlelit procession.

Since this is not Mass, the presider may be a deacon, priest, or any properly trained lay minister. Be mindful of the gestures and texts that are proper to ordained and lay persons. The *Book of Blessings* is a good resource to review for understanding the distinctions.

Order of Service

INTRODUCTORY RITE

Assuming an evening gathering, walking in procession into the worship space with candles in hand has a way of honoring us as persons and as a community. If it is another time of the day, a procession of people in solidarity with persons whose dignity is under attack is a visible sign of the right relationships to which God calls us. The beginning point for the procession might be a location of significance to the issue at hand, if feasible, or another site of import in the local community. The prayer leader greets the assembly[6] and comments briefly on the circumstances that have brought people together. Sing an opening song such as "Canticle of the Turning" by Rory Cooney (GIA), "Christ, Be Our Light" by Bernadette Farrell (OCP), or "The Summons" by John L. Bell (GIA). After the opening song, offer an opening prayer. *The Roman Missal* includes prayers for the Progress of Peoples (#29), the Preservation of Peace and Justice (#30), or For Refugees and Exiles

---

5. Refer to page 82 for an outline of Evening Prayer and a Service of the Word.

6. Use any of the greetings used for Mass, Liturgy of the Hours, or the *Book of Blessings.* Lay ministers may use those from the Hours or those for lay ministers as found in the *Book of Blessings.*

(#32) that can be adapted for the occasion. The Collects from these Masses could be used for these purposes.

LITURGY OF THE WORD

Every service should include a Liturgy of the Word, for it is where Christ speaks to us. Consider Luke 10:25–37 (Lectionary #105C) or Matthew 25:31–46 (Lectionary #160A). You should also include a Responsorial Psalm that is rooted in justice such as Psalm 15, Psalm 25, Psalm 34, or Psalm 72. A homily or reflection should follow the readings. Jesus was a storyteller, often using parables. He knew that stories gently draw us in and respect the human person and our innate capacity for stories. They shape our identity and communicate meaning. Parables are a form of story that "show the fault lines beneath the comfortable surfaces of the worlds we build for ourselves."[7] They "are agents of change and sometimes disruption."[8] No wonder Jesus told parables, and no wonder that the hearing of these texts can make us uncomfortable.

All of this is to say that the preacher will do well to honor the dignity of humanity by telling the stories of people whose dignity has been cruelly threatened and discounted. Their stories are part of the story of salvation. When their stories are put in conversation with the Word of God, they become like parables, showing the fault lines in our society, shaking us out of our complacency and bidding us to change. Resist explaining away their meaning; invite people to enter in and find themselves there.

To help the assembly reflect more deeply upon the situation, you might consider following the reflection with a period of silence or a song. Consider "Open My Eyes, Lord" by Jesse Manibusan (OCP), "The Servant Song" by Richard Gillard (various publishers), or "Make Me a Channel of Your Peace" (traditional; available from various publishers).

Adding intercessions to the service solidly connects the liturgy to the needs of the world. Look to the *General Instruction of the Roman Missal* (see 69–71) for guidance in composing the petitions. Here are a few suggestions for wording.

Refugees

For refugees forced from their homelands and fleeing in fear, may our global community respond with compassion and assist them with finding safety and shelter, we pray to the Lord.

---

7. Herbert Anderson and Edward Foley, *Mighty Stories, Dangerous Rituals: Weaving Together the Human and the Divine.* San Francisco: Jossey-Bass, 1998, 14.

8. Anderson and Foley, *Mighty Stories,* 14.

Asylum

For people who are seeking asylum, may their stories be respected, and may we receive them with hospitality, we pray to the Lord.

Human Trafficking

For the millions of victims of human trafficking throughout the world, may we act to end the enslavement of human persons and work for their freedom and flourishing, we pray to the Lord.

Racism and Prejudice

For an end to racist and prejudicial attitudes and actions and the harm inflicted by the sins of racism and ethnic hatred, may we work courageously to ensure justice for people targeted because of their race or ethnicity, we pray to the Lord.

Religious Persecution

For people who are persecuted, taunted, or threatened because of their religious beliefs and practices, may we stand in solidarity with them, we pray to the Lord.

CONCLUDING RITE

Offer the Lord's Prayer. When introducing the Lord's Prayer, use these or similar words to express unity:

Life shared in Christ compels us to share in the sufferings of all who are unjustly treated; let us pray in one voice the words Jesus gave us.

To conclude the service, again, we can look to *The Roman Missal's* prayers for the Progress of Peoples (#29), the Preservation of Peace and Justice (#30), or For Refugees and Exiles (#32) for a closing prayer that can be adapted for the occasion. The liturgy may conclude with a Prayer over the People such as numbers 2, 5, and 26 from the Missal. You might also use this original text:

May God give us courage to protect the dignity of every person and work toward a more compassionate and just world. Through Christ our Lord.

For the dismissal, use any of the four options provided in the Missal for Mass.

Singing an uplifting song rooted in the social mission of the Church would do well to conclude the service. Numerous options abound, however, you might consider "Go to the World" (traditional; various publishers), "We Are Called" by David Haas (GIA), "City of God" by Dan Schutte (WLP), or "Lift Ev'ry Voice and Sing" by James Weldon Johnson (traditional; various publishers).

Ecumenical or Interreligious Gathering

Acts against human dignity impact an entire community—local and global. A time of prayer shared with other Christians and people of other religious traditions is a powerful show of solidarity among people. There might be a procession to the place where an act of injustice occurred or is presently unfolding. Passages from sacred texts or other readings from voices in the respective traditions can be proclaimed. Testimonies or other reflections may be offered from leaders of the traditions represented. Close collaboration with the local faith leaders is a must in the preparation of an ecumenical or interreligious gathering.

Sunday Mass

The prayer texts for the Mass usually need to be used on Sundays; however, there are other opportunities to refer to and pray for this need from Sunday to Sunday. Ideas are found below.

INTRODUCTION TO THE MASS

When something happens that warrants our attention and immediate prayers and actions, mention of this need must be made at the beginning of Mass. The *General Instruction of the Roman Missal* provides presiders with the option of introducing the Mass. This is an opportunity for him (or for the liturgist) to prepare an original text that addresses particular concerns. This text precedes the Penitential Act. Consider the following example:

> We gather aware that human beings forced to leave their homes and seek safety in other countries are often met with hostility. Mindful of any actions or inactions on our part that contribute to the injustices inflicted upon refugees and migrants, let us turn to our merciful God in a moment of silence. [*Presider then invites all to pray the Penitential Act using the option found in the Missal.*]

PENITENTIAL ACT

The invocations for the Penitential Act, form III, may be adapted to address the acts against human dignity that are confronting the community. The following are examples for situations involving refugees, migrants, and those seeking asylum.

> Lord Jesus, you hear the cries of those who live in fear and journey outside their homeland to find safety and peace. Lord, have mercy.

> Christ Jesus, you know the anguish of people who are mistreated as they search for a better life. Christ, have mercy.

> Lord Jesus, you hold close the suffering and give them strength. Christ, have mercy.

Liturgy and Ministry in Times of Need

PREACHING POINTS

There are numerous statements and resources available from bishops' conferences. For example, the United States bishops have dedicated web pages to Immigration, Asylum, Migrants, Refugees and Travelers, as well as Combating Racism. Pope Francis frequently speaks about these concerns; his statements on these issues are widely available online. Also helpful are the websites of organizations that are dedicated to addressing these matters such as Catholic Charities USA and Catholic Relief Services.

But, tell the stories! Wrap the words of leaders of the Church and humanitarian organizations, scholars, and social justice ministers in the stories of the people who are suffering. Pose the tough questions: What does the Gospel call us to do in response to the terrible indignities suffered by our fellow human beings? What can we do *today* as Church in the world to combat the injustices that figuratively and too often literally put persons to death? What can we do *today* to bring these individuals to life?

EUCHARISTIC PRAYER

The presider might look to the Eucharistic Prayers for Reconciliation or Various Needs and Occasions III or VI in *The Roman Missal.*

ONGOING PRAYER

WEEKDAY AND SUNDAY MASSES

Continue to include petitions for this need at weekday and Sunday Masses. You may use those provided in this resource. When appropriate, use the Eucharistic Prayers for Various Needs and Occasions and Reconciliation and celebrate the Masses and Prayers for Various Needs and Occasions related to concerns affecting human dignity such as:

- For Promoting Harmony (#15)
- For Reconciliation (#16)
- For the Unity of Christians (#17)
- For Persecuted Christians (#19)
- For the Sanctification of Human Labor (#26)
- For the Progress of Peoples (#29)
- For the Preservation of Peace and Justice (#30)
- In the Time of War or Civil Disturbance (#31)
- For Refugees and Exiles (#32)
- In Time of Famine or for Those Suffering Hunger (#33)
- For Our Oppressors (#42)

- For Those in Captivity (#43)
- For Those in Prison (#44)
- For the Sick (#45)
- For the Dying (#46)
- For Giving Thanks to God for the Gift of Human Life (#48/1)

The Missal also includes a selection of prayers for civil needs. Although these prayers are mostly concerned with those who govern, it may be appropriate to use these prayers when praying for a change in laws or oppressive actions inflicted upon people by a regime. The Masses and Prayers for Various Needs and Occasions may be used on weekdays that do not already have an obligatory celebration, such as a feast or solemnity.

SAINTS

Celebrate the solemnities, feasts, and memorials of the saints, such as the patron saint of refugees, St. Alban, on June 22; the patron saint of immigrants, St. Frances Xavier Cabrini, on November 13; or the patron saint of victims of human trafficking, St. Josephine Bakhita, on February 8 (also the annual day of prayer and awareness against human trafficking). Recently in the United States, the Feast of Our Lady of Guadalupe on December 12 is celebrated as a day of solidarity with immigrants. The Church in the United States celebrates National Migration Week in January, which is another opportunity for a parish to gather for prayer.

PENITENTIAL SERVICES

Acts against human dignity are a matter of social sin, meaning that all of us bear some degree of responsibility, whether because of apathy or because of actions, words, or attitudes that perpetuate societal sins. With this in mind, consider a nonsacramental penitential service such as the third option found in appendix II of the Church's *Rite of Penance*. The act of repentance for this option focuses on the Beatitudes.

BLESSINGS

The *Book of Blessings* includes the Order for the Blessing of a Victim of Crime or Oppression (chapter I, part III). This blessing is highly appropriate to use with refugees, migrants, and all who are seeking asylum from oppressive conditions. For those who are actively ministering to those in oppressive conditions, especially organizations, you might also use the Order for the Blessing of Organizations Concerned with Public Need (chapter 7) and the Order for the Blessing of Those Who Exercise Pastoral Service (chapter 60).

ENVIRONMENT AND MUSIC

Attend to the racial and ethnic diversity of the parish and local community by preparing liturgical celebrations that reflect and celebrate this diversity—for example, in the art and environment of the worship space, the music, the preaching, and the language(s) in which the community sings and prays. We should also make sure that the diversity of the assembly is reflected in those who are chosen to serve as liturgical ministers.

MINISTRY AND OUTREACH

The United States bishops have been unwavering in their support of the duty of Catholics to welcome the migrant and the refugee. They affirm the rights of all peoples to migrate to sustain their lives and the lives of their families while at the same time affirming the rights of nations to secure their borders. They speak out for immigration reform in a system that is broken and in need of repair. They continually oppose actions that break up families, dividing children from their parents and husbands from their wives. The bishops are in support of family-based immigration, emphasizing that families belong together.

> Every threat to human dignity and life must necessarily be felt in the Church's very heart; it cannot but affect her at the core of her faith in the Redemptive Incarnation of the Son of God, and engage her in her mission of proclaiming the Gospel of life in all the world and to every creature (cf. Mk 16:15).
>
> —*The Gospel of Life*

In a homily during a prayer service for immigrants and refugees, Archbishop Charles Chaput said:

It's not enough for us to accept the teachings of the Church about immigration. It's important for us also to embrace those teachings in a passionate kind of way. It's important for us not to be afraid, because this is a difficult, complex, and controversial issue.[9]

Education

Part of our calling as parish leaders, as we examine the global crisis of refugees and immigrants, is to not be afraid to talk about it. It is difficult. It is complex. It is controversial. We must use our circles of influence to bring what the faithful hear every day in the news and help them make sense of it in light of Church teaching. We have a long line of Church teaching to

---

9. Homily of Archbishop Charles J. Chaput, OFM CAP, Justice for Immigrants Prayer Service, Cathedral Basilica of Sts. Peter and Paul, Philadelphia, Saturday, March 19, 2017.

stand proudly and firmly on, without fear we are becoming political. We can criticize political policies or ideas, or even an entire administration, when we know we have a strong foothold in Scripture and Tradition. We must find ways to unpack what the faithful is experiencing in their day to day lives during a homily. We must include issues of the day in the Universal Prayer. We must creatively program for the needs of the parishioners to explore the current issues in light of Catholic Social Teaching.

When it comes to acts against human dignity, we must preach about it, teach about it, and act in accordance with Church teaching to relieve those affected. In your region, what are the needs? Has your area seen an influx of Syrian refugees, or perhaps your area has a burgeoning population of migrant workers? What are the needs of these communities? English lessons may be needed for those newly arrived to your region, or perhaps food and household items may be needed as new people arrive from refugee camps overseas. Many new arrivals may be processing the trauma of persecution, war, and violence and may require counseling. Ascertain the needs of your region and your city, and look to work with established groups whose purpose is to assist new immigrants. If no such organizations exist, your parish may team with other groups or churches to establish a means of assisting those who are arriving to your area. Do not forget the youth of your parish in such assistance programming! Parish youth are filled with energy and hopeful ideology that is ideal for working with others as Christ's hands and feet.

In national and international situations that involve acts against human dignity, it is also important to look to assist those most affected. Catholic organizations such as Catholic Relief Services and many religious orders exist in regions affected by war, genocide, and refugee crises. Your parish can assist these groups in ministry by fundraising or arranging for relief services. When possible, invite religious or lay speakers who have experience working in relief services; hearing and seeing people who have personally witnessed such calamity can help people learn to understand the crises and help them learn to reach out to help others.

Day of Reflection

To help your community understand the situation, the parish may host a day of reflection to break open myths and misconceptions about immigration. We must help people move from seeing our nation through a lens of scarcity to seeing it through a lens of abundance. We fear our limitations, but as a nation we have so much to offer. A Saturday day of reflection could include Morning Prayer, a competent and knowledgeable facilitator, a delicious lunch, and a commitment to open conversation and interaction. Promote the day with "Fact or Fiction?" statements on social media, in the bulletin, and in the parish hall. Then commit to sorting out the many myths and misconceptions people carry within them surrounding migrants, or giving people the chance to build their knowledge base so they can counter a myth or two when they hear them.

Explore the myths. Ask people to list the negative stereotypes or beliefs that people hold about immigrants, whether documented or undocumented. Take time to name and unpack the fears behind belief statements such as these, countering each with facts:

- Undocumented immigrants are taking away jobs from American workers.
- Undocumented immigrants engage in criminal activity.
- Undocumented immigrants don't pay taxes.
- The Catholic Church supports illegal immigration and "open borders."
- Immigrants are a drain on the US economy.
- Undocumented immigrants are a burden on the healthcare system.
- Refugees from the Middle East are here to recruit or cause terror.
- Immigrants today don't want to learn English or to work hard.
- Undocumented immigrants enter the country illegally.

As the day finishes, take the time to bless and release all of the sadness, all of the negative energy that each belief holds. Offer pledge cards that the participants can sign for the parish and for their own purses or wallets to commit themselves to positive action. Perhaps a statement such as this will bring the day to a rightful conclusion:

I, _____, value the biblical virtue of hospitality to the migrant and stranger in my midst. I pledge from this day forward to be a positive voice for the newcomer in my community. I will speak up when I hear negative statements about a group of people being made within my social circles. I will do my best to engage in respectful conversation with others that corrects misconceptions and stereotypes. I will seek out relationships with those new to my community, with those who look different than me, worship differently than me, or act in ways that are different from what I have known. I will seek first the common dignity we all have within us as a child of God. I pledge to not live in fear of the other from this day forward.

Retreat

Another concrete idea surrounding the issue of immigration is to offer a parish retreat day for children and parents to enjoy together. Perhaps it is a morning retreat, a few hours long, centered on the lifecycle of the monarch butterfly. Find a book or movie about the monarch to introduce the insect. For example, Gail Gibbons' book *Monarch Butterfly*, appropriate for preschool through second grade, could be used to introduce the insect, and the book *The Monarch: Saving Our Most-Loved Butterfly* by Kylee Baumle, with its stunning photographs, could be an excellent accent to a day like this. There are also clips of the lifecycle of the monarch available for viewing on YouTube.com. If the facilitator can bring in milkweed or an actual chrysalis, all the better!

Monarch butterflies are the only insects that migrate each year to a warmer climate that is 2,500 miles away. This is the longest known distance for insect migration, and it has been occurring for thousands of years. Having left Canada and Minnesota in September and October, they make it to central Mexico in November and overwinter there, resting for several months before the same generation starts its return trip north. When they overwinter in Mexico, they find the same high mountain peaks—only about a dozen—and use the very same trees to roost in each and every year. This seems incredible to us, especially because these roosting butterflies aren't the same ones who were there the year prior! These are the new fourth generation butterflies. You see, no individual butterfly makes the complete round trip. Scientists know that at least four generations of Monarchs are involved in the annual cycle. Monarchs migrate primarily for two reasons: (1) they cannot withstand freezing temperatures in the northern climates, and (2) the larval food plants, the milkweed, do not grow in the overwintering sites, requiring their return north again where the plants will be plentiful. So they migrate great distances for their own survival. Encourage those attending the retreat to think about this delicate but strong creature. What propels her forward each spring and each fall? What guides her to where she needs to be? Surely, God has given this creature what it needs for survival. The answer is simple: the food they need for the larval stage, the milkweed plant, only grows in the North, in Canada and Minnesota. Yet they cannot stay there year-round, because they cannot withstand the freezing temperatures. Hence they are forced to migrate for their very survival.

Flesh out various scenarios: There are human beings who must migrate because of famine, war, terror, natural disaster, or poverty—some must leave their beloved homeland in search of work. They, too, undertake long distances for their own survival. Some take their whole family and leave permanently. Some leave with permission, others just go out of desperation and hope to get permission once they reach safety. Some send an adult parent to another country to find a job and send money back to their family who stays behind. It is not easy to go, it is not easy to stay behind, and it is not easy to be separated. It is a tough journey for everyone, and there is danger involved. Comparing these needs of the undocumented to the story of to the monarch butterfly, we realize there should be no boundaries or barriers. They are free to go where they need to go to keep themselves alive and thriving. It is not so easy, nor so simple, for the human being. Yet the words of Pope Francis ring true: "In God's heart, there are no enemies. God only has sons and daughters. We are the ones who raise walls, build barriers, and label people."[10]

During the retreat, read aloud paragraph 21 from the document *Justice in the World* issued by the World Synod of Bishops in 1971:

> Take, for example, the case of migrants. They are often forced to leave their own country to find work, but frequently find the doors closed in their faces because of discriminatory attitudes, or, if they can enter, they are often obliged to lead an insecure life or are treated in an inhuman manner.

Ask the children present what the country's role might be who is receiving an immigrant, based on what we know about why they leave, and the hardship they face. For those of us who live in the United States, ask what we might do for someone we meet who is new to our neighborhood or school, having just newly arrived from another school, city, or country to make their life just a little easier. Spend some time talking about compassion and building empathy within the children. Share the biblical virtue of hospitality and the mandates to welcome the stranger, to love our neighbor as our very selves, the Golden Rule, and so on.

See if the youth present can make some connections between an immigrant and a monarch butterfly, drawing out similarities and differences for the group. The day can finish with an art project of a monarch: a drawing, a painting, or a tissue paper artwork to symbolize and remember the journey the insect and the human both take.

---

10. Homily of Pope Francis for the Ordinary Public Consistory for the Creation of New Cardinals, St. Peter's Basilica; November 19, 2016.

CONCLUSION

As I think about where we are lucky or unlucky enough to be born, combined with the unequal distribution of the world's goods and resources, unbridled consumerism, the rule of evil dictators, and how quickly war can break out or a natural disaster can strike, I'm reminded how very vulnerable and fragile each of our lives are. I am convinced that today, more than ever, we are to work for the common good, not simply our own self-interests, and that the common good has to extend beyond the borders of our own nation. I shudder at a haunting verse from Scripture: "Those who shut their ears to the cry of the poor / will themselves call out and not be answered" (Proverbs 21:13), and I try to heed the words from Psalm 15: "Whoever walks without blame, / doing what is right, / speaking truth from the heart; / Who does not slander with his tongue, / does no harm to a friend, / never defames a neighbor" (15:2–3).

> There are many things that can only be seen through eyes that have cried.
>
> —St. Oscar Romero

CHAPTER TWO

Acts of Violence

"Love your enemies, and pray for those who persecute you."

—Matthew 5:44

THEOLOGICAL AND SOCIAL CONTEXT

The Sandy Hook Elementary School shooting occurred on December 14, 2012, in Newtown, Connecticut, when a twenty-year-old first fatally shot his mother, and then drove to his former school and shot and killed twenty young children between six and seven years old, and six adult staff members. Elementary school children! I try to place myself among these mothers and fathers, these grandparents, teachers, and siblings. I try to imagine being the mother who sent my son or daughter off to school with a quick hug and a kiss on a winter day, in the midst of both the stress and anticipation of the holiday season. I cannot imagine. But, in truth, I don't want to imagine. I don't want to know the horror and absolute devastation of these parents whose arms ache to hold their children still today, who now only look at pictures of past birthday parties and watch old videos in order to remember the sound of their child's laughter. I don't want to be the mom who rifles through clumsy art projects and mother's day cards, who stands and looks around in a hollow bedroom and sees an empty seat at the dinner table, who tries to imagine what their little one would look like or be doing in the present day. And I don't want to imagine the pain that the shooter's father knows either, left to grapple each day with the fact that his own son could have been capable of such violence. This was a horrific act of violence whose destruction knows no end.

And we know that the list of violence goes on. Along with acts of terror and gun violence that dominate the news, I think of the quiet violence that goes on daily, the violence that is underreported and therefore hidden from so many. How many women suffer domestic violence in this nation and around the globe, terrified of daily life with their partner and unable to break free from a destructive pattern of violence? Perhaps she lacks the resources or the confidence, or is paralyzed by the fear and the very real threat has been repeated to her over and over that if she makes a move, her partner will find out and kill her or, worse yet, her children. And so she stays.

I think, too, of the number of women and girls who are raped, kidnapped, and sold for the sex trade, and are victim-survivors of sexual violence each year. Rape and sexual assault remain a largely underreported crime, especially on college campuses. When faced with the daunting prospect of separate investigations both on campus and in the legal system, along with feelings of shame and the possibility of either being blamed or not being believed, many women choose to just get back to "normal life" and resume classes and activities without telling anyone what happened.

In his homily at the Vigil of Prayer for Peace on September 7, 2013, Pope Francis spoke of the chaos that results when the harmony that God intends is not honored by human action. He laments:

It is exactly in this chaos that God asks the man's conscience, "Where is Abel your brother?" and Cain responds, "I do not know; am I my brother's keeper?" (Genesis 4:9). We too are asked this question; it would be good for us to ask ourselves as well: am I really my brother's keeper? Yes, you are your brother's keeper! To be human means to care for one another! But when harmony is broken, a metamorphosis occurs: the brother who is to be cared for and loved becomes an adversary to fight and kill. What violence occurs at that moment, how many conflicts, how many wars have marked our history! We need only look at the suffering of so many brothers and sisters. This is not a question of coincidence, but the truth: we bring about the rebirth of Cain in every act of violence and in every war. All of us! . . . As if it were normal, we continue to sow destruction, pain, death!

I think the haunting point our Holy Father is making here is that we are all responsible for the well-being of each other, and when one member of the Body of Christ is suffering, we all suffer. We all suffer for the wounded and the dead in the mass shootings and for those who love them, and we all have a responsibility for the well-being of the person who pulled the trigger or set off the explosion. We are responsible for the abused and for the abuser, for the victim survivor as well as the rapist. We are our sister's and brother's keeper as she or he seeks belonging, security, acceptance, love, and basic needs that include healthcare and mental health services in today's society. That is a tough thing to realize and to own, and we don't want to sit with that possibility too long because it makes us uncomfortable. It is much easier to write off the shooter as a "crazy person" than to take a hard look at the fabric of our society and honestly name and claim where mental health, gun laws, bullying, personal interactions, and public policy have poorly intersected and what "my" personal responsibility is in these situations. And as Pope Francis rightly points out, acts of violence have become more and more normalized in today's world and we, in turn, are in danger of becoming increasingly numb to the horrific news we hear each day. We let it wash over us as we make the commute home or do the evening's dishes and do not dwell with the tragedy too long, not internalizing it in a significant way, knowing a new one will be in the next day's news. We are a society who is becoming immune to the suffering of others and who is losing the capacity for empathy. We are weary.

> **The Catholic community is in a position to respond to violence and the threat of violence in our society with new commitment and creativity.**
>
> —*Confronting a Culture of Violence: A Catholic Framework for Action*

The United States bishops have long called for greater gun control measures in our nation, believing that weapons that are increasingly capable of inflicting great suffering in a short period of time are simply too accessible (see *A Mercy and Peacebuilding Approach to Gun Violence*, March 2018). After a gunman killed seventeen people at a Florida high school in 2018, Cardinal Blase Cupich of Chicago wrote strongly, "Let us make it clear to our elected officials that the weapons and ammunition that facilitate this carnage have no place in our culture." Advocating for the regulation of firearms is consistent with the Church's promotion of peace at home and around the world, and for its message of life. A comprehensive pastoral statement addressing gun violence was issued in 1994 by the United States bishops, titled *Confronting a Culture of Violence: A Catholic Framework for Action* and since then its leaders have followed up with many statements calling for reasonable measures to address gun violence, including universal background checks, limitations on high capacity weapons and ammunition magazines, increased resources for mental health care, and a call in 2000 to ban the sale of most handguns except for law enforcement and the military. In so many ways, the Church is taking a prophetic, countercultural stance on this issue. Yet there are also voices among us calling for greater security in various forms, in an effort to feel safer amidst the violence that surrounds us. It might be at our airports or schools, in the strengthening of our police forces, or in the arming of citizens with the enactment of conceal and carry laws. In the *Joy of the Gospel* (59), Pope Francis challenges that notion when he argues:

> [U]ntil exclusion and inequality in society and between peoples are reversed, it will be impossible to eliminate violence. The poor and poorer peoples are accused of violence, yet without equal opportunities the different forms of aggression and conflict will find a fertile terrain for growth and eventually explode. When a society—whether local, national, or global—is willing to leave a part of itself on the fringes, no political programs or resources spent on law enforcement or surveillance systems can indefinitely guarantee tranquility. This is not the case simply because inequality provokes a violent reaction from those excluded from the system, but because the socioeconomic system is unjust at its root.

These words remind me of how Americans grappled with the aftermath of the September 11 terrorist attacks. Beyond the shock, the fear, the sadness and disbelief that surrounded those first days and weeks after the terror attacks, there was a bit of an awakening, even a loss of innocence in our nation. For many, it was the first time they realized that some in the world did not like their country or way of life, and they needed to grapple with why that was so. Francis' words can help put into perspective how our society has most definitely marginalized and excluded many, and with the passing of time we can better see how violent reactions continually erupt from those who are kept on the fringes, whether that be from the terrorists in 9/11 or a school shooter.

As those who live with an abundance go about their lives oblivious to those who have nothing, there is a cost. It reminds me of the story in the Gospel according to Luke, where the chilling parable of the Rich Man and Lazarus is recounted (see Luke 16:19–31). The rich man did nothing to intentionally harm another, rather his was a sin of omission. He dined sumptuously each day and dressed well, and was completely oblivious to the beggar lying outside his door, covered in sores, whose name was Lazarus. It's fascinating to me who has a name in this story and who does not! The rich man did not hurt Lazarus but of course he did nothing to help lift Lazarus up from the miserable condition from which he found himself living day to day, either. The story goes on to say that upon their deaths, the rich man finds himself in torment, in eternal damnation, whereas Lazarus entered Paradise. Separating the two of them is a great chasm that cannot be crossed, which the rich man realizes after he begs Abraham to send Lazarus to dip his finger in water to cool his tongue. The rich man is denied this request and told that while he enjoyed what was good in his lifetime and Lazarus received what was bad, now the tables have been turned (see Luke 16:19–31). This parable gives many from developed nations reason to pause each Sunday it is proclaimed during liturgy, and perhaps have it strike a bit of fear in our hearts. It is a challenging Gospel that should bother us as we examine our lives and our relationship with the poor at our door. Certainly, the conditions necessary for a sustainable and peaceful existence with all other living creatures on this planet have a long way to go in order to attain the harmony that God envisions for all of us, not just some of us.

Another layer of tragedy with the acts of violence we have witnessed is that so many of the terrorist attacks have opened up a vast quantity of fear, namely "fear of the other." This "other" could be anyone who speaks with an accent, or has skin that is darker than mine, or who practices a religion that I know little or nothing about. This fear of the other has been especially targeted toward our sisters and brothers who are Muslim. It seems that after 9/11, many of our Muslim sisters and brothers hold their breath whenever they hear of another act of violence, hoping it will not be a religious extremist that distorts the belief systems of Islam and brings further suspicion and marginalization upon them—women, men, and children who are already expending enormous amounts of energy each day trying to assimilate in a culture that is not their own.

In *The Joy of the Gospel* (252), Pope Francis reflects:

Our relationship with the followers of Islam has taken on greater importance, since they are now significantly present in many traditionally Christian countries, where they can freely worship and become fully a part of society. We must never forget that they 'profess to hold the faith of Abraham, and together with us they adore the one, merciful God, who will judge humanity on the last day' [*Dogmatic Constitution on the Church*, 16]. . . . [I]t is admirable to see how Muslims both young and old, men and women, make time for daily prayer and faithfully take part in religious services. Many of them also have a deep conviction that their life, in its entirety, is from God and for God. They also acknowledge the need to respond to God with an ethical commitment and with mercy toward those most in need.

Along with these virtues and the reminder that Christians and Muslims (and Jews for that matter) worship the same God, Pope Francis goes on to caution us to not make generalizations or stereotypes about people who are Muslim: "Faced with disconcerting episodes of violent fundamentalism, our respect for true followers of Islam should help us to avoid hateful generalizations, for authentic Islam and the proper reading of the Koran are opposed to every form of violence" (*The Joy of the Gospel*, 253). So if a media outlet, or a fellow Christian, is going on with misconceptions about Islam, it is our duty to change the channel or respectfully correct our sister or brother.

LITURGY AND PRAYER

"Thoughts and prayers." Sadly, the frequency with which we hear or see these words in response to an act of violence has nearly worn them into a trite sentiment. Some voices suggest that the words are empty if not accompanied by sincere actions leading to change.

For people of faith, prayer—both personal and communal—is a necessary response to monstrous acts. Prayer keeps us from turning away from the human suffering resulting from such acts, and in fact, increases our capacity to share in these sufferings. It stretches our hearts and minds so we can imagine life-giving possibilities for a world in need of transformation. Prayer emboldens us to work for change and compels us to act—whether this means to advocate for changes in the law, protest unjust social structures, provide comfort and assistance to victims and survivors, or take a number of other actions. In this way, we give visible witness to who we are—the Body of Christ.

The pervasive nature of acts of violence—in homes and workplaces, in our neighborhoods and cities, within a nation and between nations, nearby and far away, one death or injured person or large scale events—calls us to *persistent* prayer. A single prayer event in the immediate aftermath of a horrific act of violence is the opening event. The prevalence of violence in our time calls for keeping vigil with recurring, resolute prayer. Maybe then, as God's grace repeatedly washes over us, shaping us into Christ's image; as we surrender to the healing and renewing power of the Holy Spirit, the transformation that is needed will take hold.

> The Sunday eucharist, therefore, not only does not absolve the faithful from the duties of charity, but on the contrary commits them even more "to all the works of charity, of mercy, of apostolic outreach, by means of which it is seen that the faithful of Christ are not of this world and yet are the light of the world, giving glory to the Father in the midst of [the people]."
>
> —*The Day of the Lord*, 69

IMMEDIATE RESPONSE

Acts of violence affect everyone. Depending on the makeup of the local community, it is fitting to prepare a time of communal prayer that is ecumenical and/or interreligious as an immediate response to acts of violence. We also need to be ready to welcome all who desire to participate, regardless of religious belief.

Ecumenical Gathering

A form of communal prayer that has broad appeal among Christians is that of the Taizé community, an ecumenical monastic community devoted to prayer and reconciliation. Taizé prayer can be adapted by Christian communities and is especially appropriate for ecumenical gatherings. Close collaboration with our Christian sisters and brothers in our neighborhoods and wider communities is, of course, essential to creating a prayer experience in the tradition of Taizé. Representatives from the various communities who will be involved with preparing the prayer service should work together to discern song selections and Scripture readings, and write intercessions and other prayer texts.

You will need to consider the needs of the assembly. Will the time of prayer draw those touched by violence—victims and survivors, their family members or friends? Will leaders of the local community be present? Will there be first responders and others who have been immediately involved with attending to the wounded and dead be present? How might the parish extend hospitality to all of these individuals? How will the leadership of the prayer and particular liturgical roles be shared among the representatives of the Christian communities that participate?

Once it is decided which of the participating Christian communities will host the prayer service, the worship space might be prepared with a prominent cross or icon of Christ, subdued lighting and candles.

ORDER OF SERVICE

A key resource for creating a prayer service in the tradition of the Taizé is the Taizé community's website, particularly their "At the Wellspring of Faith" page: https://www.taize.fr/en_rubrique43.html. The site includes psalms, readings, and intercessions for each day, as well as guidance on preparing a time of prayer. The framework for communal prayer found there is:

- Psalm
- Reading
- Song
- Silence
- Intercessions or litany of praise
- Our Father
- Concluding prayer
- Song

This framework can be adapted to include a call to worship that would serve to welcome the participants, acknowledge the act of violence that has prompted the event, and provide any necessary instructions. The call to worship may be followed by a song of the Taizé community, such as "Holy Spirit, Come to Us."[1]

Scripture passages to consider for a prayer service in response to acts of violence are 2 Corinthians 4:7–15; Romans 12:9–16; Ephesians 4:25–32; Philippians 2:1–11. A reflection from one of the representatives of the Christian communities may be added after the reading. It could be an opportunity to tell the stories of those who have died or are injured or grieving, if these stories are known. The preacher might tap the writings, speeches, or homilies of individuals who have spoken out against violence, including those who themselves were victims of violence, like Martin Luther King, Jr. and Oscar Romero. Further, it would be a time to call upon Christians to carry out their baptismal responsibilities to be ministers of peace and justice in the world.

Silence is integral to prayer and should be incorporated throughout the prayer service. As beautifully described by the Taizé community, "Silence makes us ready for a new meeting with God. In silence, God's Word can reach the hidden corners of our hearts."[2]

Interreligious Gathering

Responding to acts of violence is also an opportunity for people of various religious backgrounds to gather for ritual, reflection, and strengthening relationships within the local community. Once again, collaboration in preparing an interreligious gathering is critical to ensure that everyone feels welcomed and invited to engage in the time of prayer. You will need to prepare texts and music that appeal to all who will be attending. Consider if the gathering will include victims and survivors of violence and their

---

1. For the songs and prayers of the Taizé community, visit GIA Publications, www.giamusic.com.
2. "The Value of Silence," accessed on the Taizé community web site at https://www.taize.fr /en_article12.html.

family members or friends; leaders of the local community; first responders and others who provided assistance to victims. You will also need to consider how your parish will welcome all of these individuals to participate and how the leadership of the service will be shared among the representatives of the religious traditions.

For interreligious gatherings, it might be preferable to find an outdoor location or another site where people of different religious traditions feel comfortable. This is not to say that a place of worship is never appropriate, but the location requires input from all the religious leaders who will be involved. For subsequent gatherings, perhaps the faith communities can take turns hosting the time of prayer. Welcoming one another in our sacred spaces can further erase misconceptions and break down barriers to relationships. Another possibility is for people to gather for a procession to a representative site, be it the place of a mass shooting, an act of terrorism, or an area of a city where there has been a rash of violent incidences. The German theologian Karl Rahner, SJ, called processions "a holy movement of those truly united."[3] Imagine a procession of people of various religious traditions in response to acts of violence that threaten the community at large. Whether in silence or singing or proclaiming holy words, such a procession would be a powerful symbol of people "truly united."

Consider this outline for the parts of the service:

- A call to prayer and invocation from each of the traditions represented
- Readings from the sacred texts of the traditions
- Reflection offered by one or more of the religious leaders present
- Song
- Intercessions
- Sending forth
- Song or silent departure

Sunday Mass

CANTOR ANNOUNCEMENT

When the cantor invites the assembly to join in the singing of the opening song, he or she may include a reference to the act(s) of violence and invite the assembly to a time of silence before standing and singing.

---

3. Karl Rahner, *The Great Church Year: The Best of Karl Rahner's Homilies, Sermons, and Meditations*, ed. Albert Raffelt, ed. of translation Harvey D. Egan, SJ (New York: Crossroad, 1993), 228.

PREACHING POINTS

The alarming frequency of acts of violence in our society is numbing for many people. Some feel a heightened sense of fear, while others have lapsed into apathy, thinking there is nothing they can do to change any of it. A challenge for the preacher is both to reassure and to mobilize. Our reassurance and courage comes through God-with-us in Jesus Christ and the Holy Spirit. At the same time, Christians are charged to carry out the mission of the Gospel and be Eucharist to a world in need of consolation, healing, and transformation of attitudes, behaviors, and relationships. How do we live out these responsibilities in response to acts of violence in our communities, local and global? What concrete actions are we called to as individuals and as a faith community? The dismissal rite gives us our mandate—"Go and announce the Gospel of the Lord." What will we do this day, this week, to act upon this mandate and stand up to the violence that plagues our society and obscures the goodness and sacredness of our communities? What will change because we have together broken bread and shared in the cup of suffering?

INTERCESSIONS

As referenced elsewhere, for inspiration in composing intercessions, we can look to resources such as *How to Write the Prayer of the Faithful* (LTP), *Liturgy and Discipleship: Preparing Worship That Inspires and Transforms* (LTP), and *The Prayer of the Faithful: Intercessions for Your Faith Community for Years A, B, and C* (LTP). Here are a few suggestions for wording:

Domestic Violence

For families who struggle with strained or broken relationships, may they find the support they need to forgive one another and live in harmony, we pray:

For all victims of domestic violence, that they find healing for their physical and emotional wounds and safe places to live, we pray:

For our parish and civic community, that we respond to the ongoing needs of victims and survivors and work to eliminate violence within the home, we pray:

Acts of Violence on Our Streets and in Our Neighborhoods

For the children, women, and men who have been injured or who have died because of gun violence or other forms of violence in our [*community/ town/city/nation/world*], that they be received into God's loving embrace and their families and friends be comforted, we pray:

For those responsible for these acts of violence, may they come to know God's mercy and may their lives be transformed through God's love, we pray:

Mass Shootings and Acts of Terrorism

For all who died in [*identify the incident*], may their lives be honored, and may they be drawn into the heart of God, we pray:

For all who were harmed physically and emotionally in [*identify the incident*], may their wounds, both seen and unseen, be healed, and may God grant them courage and strength, we pray:

For leaders in our communities, nation, and world, may they carry out their responsibilities to protect the people they serve, we pray:

PREPARATION OF THE GIFTS

Parishioners might be asked to bring money and, if the act of violence has had a local impact, bring items needed by those directly affected. If the incident is not local, consider a donation out of the collection to national or international organizations that are responding to the needs of victims and survivors.

MUSIC

Consider including a song after Communion such as "From the Many, Make Us One" by Gabe Huck and Tony Alonso (GIA), "Make Me a Channel of Your Peace" based on the Prayer of St. Francis and adapted by Sebastian Temple (various publishers) or John Angotti (WLP), "Will the Circle be Unbroken," by Tony Alonso (GIA), or "Ubi Caritas" by Bob Hurd (OCP).

ONGOING PRAYER

As mentioned, the prevalence of violence in our local communities, nation, and world calls for resolute prayer that changes minds and hearts and inspires action. How might a parish "keep vigil"—that is, keep before the community the undeniable need for prayer and action and draw them into this effort? A few possibilities are provided below.

Weekday and Sunday Masses

It is not enough to include petitions for this need once. We need to continually remind parishioners of the need to pray for those affected by violence. We need to continually preach on these matters in a way that inspires and challenges all to live the Gospel of peace and love. Continue to adapt the Penitential Act, form III, with invocations particular to this need. When appropriate, use the Eucharistic Prayers for Various Needs and Occasions and Reconciliation and celebrate the Masses and Prayers for Various Needs and Occasions such as:

- For Promoting Harmony (#15)
- For Reconciliation (#16)
- For the Unity of Christians (#17)
- For Persecuted Christians (#19)
- For the Progress of Peoples (#29)
- For the Preservation of Peace and Justice (#30)
- In the Time of War or Civil Disturbance (#31)
- For Our Oppressors (#42)

Also recognize these needs on particular saints' days such as St. Agnes (January 21), St. Rita of Cascia (May 22), St. Maria Goretti (July 6), and St. Michael (September 29).

Stations of the Cross

Adapt the Stations of the Cross in a way that speaks to the prevalence of violence. Short meditations on the consequences of violence, both personal and societal, and the urgent need for action, healing, reconciliation, and transformation can be read during each station. The Stations of the Cross can also be adapted for ecumenical gatherings in a church or for processions with a cross to various sites in a town or city. For example, in the Archdiocese of Chicago, Cardinal Blase J. Cupich led a Stations of the Cross processing to places where victims of gun violence had fallen to their death. This took place on Good Friday. Keep in mind that Stations of the Cross, while popular during the season of Lent and Triduum, is not limited to these seasons.[4]

Pilgrimages

A pilgrimage is usually associated with traveling to a recognized sacred site, often outside of one's daily surroundings. However, we are a pilgrim people who are accompanying one another on the journey of daily life. Walking together as an act of prayer, as a way of honoring the sacred sites

---

4. For inspiration, see for example *The Way of the Cross Led by His Holiness Pope Francis* (http://www. vatican.va/news_services/liturgy/2019/documents/ns_lit_doc_20190419_via-crucis-meditazioni _en.html), *The Scriptural Stations of the Cross* (http://www.usccb.org/prayer-and-worship/prayers -and-devotions/stations-of-the-cross/scriptural-stations-of-the-cross.cfm), and the *CRS Rice Bowl Stations of the Cross* (https://www.crsricebowl.org/wp-content/uploads/2017/10/17US676-Stations -of-the-Cross-ENG.pdf). See also *A Light for My Path: Praying the Psalms on the Way of the Cross* by Michael Ruzicki (LTP). This fresh approach to the stations connects excerpts from the Book of Psalms to Christ's Passion. The contemporary illustrations reflect issues currently facing our urban communities.

where people have died because of violence, as an expression of grief but also a statement of resilience can be a transformative experience. Relationships can be formed. Others in the wider community may spontaneously and seamlessly merge with the group of pilgrims. Such pilgrimages would be a striking witness to our faith and hope in Christ.

Blessings

The *Book of Blessings* includes orders of prayer for those who have been affected by violence. Consider using the Order for the Blessing of a Victim of Crime or Oppression with a person who has been raped, abused, shot, or was the victim of another violent crime (chapter I, part III). The rite recognizes that "the personal experience of a crime . . . can be traumatic and not easily forgotten. A victim often needs the assistance of others, and no less that of God, in dealing with this experience" (*Book of Blessings*, 430). It may be led by a deacon, priest, or lay person. Although this order of prayer may take place within the parish community, the comfort of the victim should be considered first.

Night Prayer (Compline)

Introduce parishioners to Night Prayer from the Church's Liturgy of the Hours. It might, for example, be a way for all evening activities at the parish to end as a means of "keeping vigil" to bring an end to violence in our world. Compline includes an examination of conscience, which in this case might be the following:[5]

> **Briefly consider your day**: In what ways did I act to promote a more just and peaceful community? Praise God for the courage in these moments. In what ways did I miss an opportunity to contribute to a more just and peaceful community? Ask God for forgiveness and strength.

MINISTRY AND OUTREACH

When we watch the news, we regularly hear of violence in all parts of our country. People always hope that such violence cannot touch their communities, and people often tell themselves that their towns and cities are immune to violence; it is easier to pretend that it can't happen here. Still others see violence suffocating their neighborhoods and regions; violence and death permeate their daily lives and they live in fear of stray bullets striking themselves or loved ones. What happens when such violence strikes your community, and your parishioners are gravely impacted?

---

5. Refer to page 82 in this resource for an outline of Night Prayer.

Parish ministries should make themselves known to those impacted by violent acts. Affected people will be operating while in shock, and they may not consider calling their parishes while in such a state. It is important for the hurting people to be aware that ministers are present to walk with them through this difficult time. It is important that ministers prepare themselves to walk through pain and grief with their community members; the pain and grief may or may not be shared personally, but through empathetic listening, ministers can walk with the hurting faithful. It is important to listen to the people, hear their stories, and witness their grief. Telling their stories can help many people begin to walk the painful path toward healing. Ministers should not be afraid of their pain, and not be afraid to help them name their grief, mourning, and losses.

Active Listening

Ministers, especially inexperienced ministers, should learn and practice active listening skills. Active listeners hear and listen, and show their comprehension. They do not interrupt or insist that their own assumptions must be true about another person's grief. When a person is listening empathetically he or she can be with a person in his or her grief, while not taking that grief upon himself or herself. Ministers who are newly learning active listening skills can be trained to avoid using platitudes such as "we don't understand this situation now, but God knows best, and he called your loved one home" or "God needed your loved one in heaven."

> What we believe, where we are, and how we live out our faith can make a great difference in the struggle against violence. . . . We must confront this growing culture of violence with a commitment to life, a vision of hope and a call to action.
>
> —Confronting a Culture of Violence: A Catholic Framework for Action

Preaching and Adult Faith Formation

When tragedy strikes a community, particularly a tragedy that involves acts of violence, ministers find themselves in the difficult position of preaching in the name of Christ, who taught radical forgiveness, while ministering to a community that is suffering acutely from deliberate violence of one person or group toward another. A minister can address that divide by recognizing that a violent act is not the fault of an ethnic or religious group, but rather the doing of a person or persons. Forgiveness is something that may happen over time; it may not happen that day, in that period of prayer. Ministers can actively speak against vengefulness, while maintaining normal defense of oneself, one's family, and community from harm. We must maintain the human dignity of all persons, as we are all made in God's own image and likeness.

Since acts of violence pervade our nation, ongoing outreach and educational opportunities are desperately needed in our parish communities. Pastors and deacons should make a concerted effort to preach about the issue in light of the Gospel and Catholic social teaching. Adult faith formation sessions should take place breaking open the Gospel stories and Catholic social teaching as well as recent Church statements about gun violence and other issues. Catholic social teaching should be taught in Catholic schools and religions education sessions. Parish justice and education staff (intergenerational formation) should coordinate outreach actions with the liturgical and education efforts.

Contacting Lawmakers

Parishioners could be asked to call or write postcards after Mass to lawmakers about the issue, and even visit legislators to share their concerns about how this type of violence is affecting their families and communities. A march could be organized that listed the names of all who have fallen victim to violence. Organize a speaker or panel that will help increase understanding of the cultural and religious practices of our sisters and brothers who are Muslim. Questions can be asked about the practice of prayer, fasting, and foot washing, the role of women and why some women are covered, how the prophet Muhammed and the Koran came to be, and misconceptions surrounding the concept of *jihad*, or holy war. With greater understanding comes appreciation and the possibility of a relationship. And wherever there is relationship, the call to love our neighbor as ourselves, as mandated in the Gospel, becomes so much easier.

Prayer Intentions

A simple outreach a parish community can be encouraged to do in the immediate aftermath of a tragedy that happens anywhere in the world is to invite parishioners to write their prayers on a makeshift wall. The idea takes little to no time or preparation on the part of the pastoral staff: simply hang a very long sheet of roll paper in a high-traffic area such as the narthex or parish center and title it "Our Prayers for N._____" and leave a basket of markers or even tempera paint nearby. Encourage people to express what's on their heart through prayerful sentiment or symbolic image, almost graffiti style. Not only is the act of stopping and expressing something at the wall healing for the individual, but it will be a reflective and prayerful place for many in the community who pause to read and absorb the thoughts and emotions of so many of those around them. The paper wall can eventually be rolled up and mailed off to the community that is hurting.

Prayer Chain

Parishes might sponsor a prayer chain that will be given to the hurting community. Invite parish members as well as members from the wider community—anyone your parish leadership perceives is hurting and in need of healing action—for an evening of prayer and healing. After a welcome and opening remarks about why you are gathered, explain that much of the evening will proceed in relative silence. Give everyone strips of paper, cut in uniform length and width. Consider taking legal-sized paper and slicing it into strips at least two inches wide. With quiet music playing, invite those gathered to write a prayer to God for the victims of the violence. When finished, invite them to sit and meditate in prayerful silence. When all are finished, a prayer gong can be rung for each victim who lost their life in the violence. Then invite those gathered to work together to glue their prayer strip onto someone else's, using as few words as possible, creating paper chain links symbolizing the unity and bond of a praying community. The group can then stand in a large circle holding the paper chain and softly singing a song such as "Peace Is Flowing Like a River." At the end of the evening, the prayer chain can be carefully boxed up and mailed to victims, to let them know that other communities care and are praying for them.

Memorials

Parish communities who are near the site of where the violence occurred can be on the front lines of initiating and maintaining a memorial site for the victims of tragedy. People need ritual, an action to do as well as a place to visit, where they can remember, be quiet and reflective, and also grieve with others who are hurting. These are the places where photos, candles, and other mementos are left. A parish could be proactive by choosing a site that makes sense, showing up early and providing votive candles and matches in large quantities, or perhaps markers and a medium such as clay, paper, yarn, or ribbon for people to create something as they arrive. Having a basket with small stones and markers nearby might be just the impetus to allow an unprepared mourner a much needed act of ritual.

Direct Outreach

Direct outreach from one community to another might also be appropriate. If the parish community is in close proximity to where the violence occurred, there will be a need for clothing, food, or blood donations. Parish communities can organize a blood bank, or clothing and food donations. Depending on the type of community it is, there might be a way to deliver homemade meals or at least get gift cards to grocery stores or restaurants to victim's families. If a large-scale explosion happens where many are left homeless, a parish can house families and ask its parishioners to prayerfully consider doing the same.

In any situation, there is always a financial need, as one considers the cumulative effect of missed work, medical bills, and perhaps legal bills from a tragedy, so consider a second collection or a parish fundraiser that would benefit a victim's family or even a victim's advocacy group. Financial donations can be shared easily across the miles from a faith community who is far away but is feeling moved to action.

Symbolic Actions

Symbolic actions that show solidarity should also be considered by faith communities. When Christchurch, New Zealand, had two mosques attacked in March 2019, and fifty worshipers were killed by a gunman espousing white nationalist beliefs, the country came together to mourn and to show respect for the Muslim community that makes up just one percent of the New Zealand population. Prime Minister Jacinda Ardern spoke powerful statements of compassion while wearing a black headscarf, and thousands of other non-Muslim women followed her lead to show solidarity with the Muslim community. A symbolic gesture like that can mean so much to the victims of the attack, and was praised by imam Gamal Fouda: "Thank you for holding our families close and honoring us with a simple scarf."[6] Our parish communities can look for similar, equally powerful gestures that show solidarity and uplift human dignity when tragedy strikes.

CONCLUSION

In the wake of a violent act, parish communities are called to grow seeds of compassion. Call forth the carpenters from the faith community to build a raised bed, have children paint it, invite many gloved hands to mix fertilizer together with rich topsoil— perhaps soil brought and shared from individual homes—and then prayerfully proclaim the Beatitudes while sowing seeds of compassion. The seeds should become something lovely: perhaps a blooming annual such as zinnias which will bring joy for many months when watered and lifted to the sun. The seeds of compassion are intentionally and prayerfully sown for the victims of violence as well as for the

> Be strong and steadfast. . . . The LORD . . . will be with you and will never fail you or forsake you.
>
> So do not fear or be dismayed.
>
> —Deuteronomy 31:7, 8

---

6. Jennifer Williams, "New Zealanders Have Sent a Clear Message to the Mosque Shooter: You Will Not Divide Us," March 22, 2019, vox.com.

perpetrators of the violence, and the prayers of all gathered have a ripple effect into the universe, truly affecting peace and goodness in our land.

In times of tragedy, when it feels as if violence is closing in on all sides, we pray in earnest with the psalmist:

My soul yearns and pines
for the courts of the LORD.
My heart and flesh cry out
for the living God. (Psalm 84:3)

May we be the living God for one another in times of need.

CHAPTER THREE

Environmental and Natural Disasters

The LORD God then took the man and settled him in the garden of
Eden, to cultivate and care for it.

—Genesis 2:15

THEOLOGICAL AND SOCIAL CONTEXT

I admit rather sheepishly that I wasn't familiar with the word *tsunami*
until March 11, 2011. On that day, the images of what happened to the
people of Japan were forever seared in my mind. A magnitude 9 undersea
earthquake happened off the northeast coast of Japan's main island in the
mid-afternoon. Less than an hour later, the quake initiated a series of large
tsunami ocean waves, some reaching heights of 133 feet and traveling inland
for 6 miles, flooding approximately 217 square miles of the country. The
tsunami caused a cooling system failure at a power station along the coast,
resulting in a level 7 nuclear meltdown of three reactors and the release of
radioactive materials into the environment. The quake triggered a series of
horrifying and destructive events, and was a surprise that few scientists
had predicted. Although not the largest or the deadliest quake in the world,
it was the most powerful in Japan, leaving 15,894 people dead, mostly from
drowning, as well as over 2,500 missing. With damage to roads and rail-
ways, a dam collapse, along with many fires, the quake also left over 4.4

million households without electricity, 1.5 million homes without water, and over 6,000 people injured. This was a natural disaster of an incredible proportion. Six years later, in 2017, residents were still recovering: 150,000 evacuees had lost their homes and 50,000 were still living in temporary housing.[1] Yet the rest of the world went on with their lives, as the story fell out of the media in a month or so after the disaster, as all stories do.

My parish included the people of Japan in the Universal Prayer for several consecutive weeks and took up a second collection with money going to Catholic Relief Services, the international humanitarian agency for the Catholic community in the United States. It seems when disasters of this magnitude strike somewhere in our globe, these are the basic things a parish community can do in response. Moved to tears, my donation felt both sacrificial and so meager at the same time.

In his apostolic exhortation *Rejoice and Be Glad*, Pope Francis claims that knowing how to mourn with others is an act of holiness. As parish communities, we can help teach and form people in compassion and empathy, and to name that as holy. Francis reasons:

A person who sees things as they truly are and sympathizes with pain and sorrow is capable of touching life's depths and finding authentic happiness. He or she is consoled, not by the world, but by Jesus. Such persons are unafraid to share in the suffering of others; they do not flee from painful situations. They discover the meaning of life by coming to the aid of those who suffer, understanding their anguish and bringing relief. . . . They feel compassion for others in such a way that all distance vanishes. (76)

Would that we all could do this when we encounter suffering, rather than the numbness of indifference we too often experience when we hear of the suffering masses, or yet another disaster or tragedy!

Another natural disaster is the devastation the people of Puerto Rico experienced from Hurricane Maria, a category 5 hurricane that also struck the United States Virgin Islands and Dominica in September 2017. It was the worst natural disaster on record to affect those islands, and the deadliest Atlantic hurricane since Hurricane Jeanne in 2004. Puerto Rico, in particular, is still in disarray with its residents experiencing obstacles to healthcare, unreliable electricity, and many still living under tarps. Long periods of time passed with residents going without not only electricity, but also water, phone service, and medical care. Imagine! These challenges, along with mismatched systems in hospitals and morgues, high rates of

---

1. See Becky Oskin, "Japan Earthquake & Tsunami of 2011: Facts and Information," September 13, 2017, LiveScience.com; accessed March 22, 2019.

Liturgy and Ministry in Times of Need

migration by those displaced by the storm, and inconclusive debate over what "counted" as a hurricane-related death makes it difficult to estimate the actual death toll, but estimates range between 3,000 and 4,600.

On August 29, 2005, Hurricane Katrina devastated New Orleans, Louisiana, and the surrounding areas. Katrina's death toll is counted at 1,800 people, and similar to Puerto Rico, there was also a mass migration of displaced residents, with New Orleans losing half of its population from the storm. With the failure of over fifty levees and flood walls, the residents of New Orleans were also victim to tens of billions of gallons of waters flooding the city and its suburbs. Yes, the storm was big, and some levees were simply overcome. However, there were other key levees in the heart of the city, such as the Seventeenth Street and London Avenue levees, that failed with water much below what they were designed to withstand. Tens of thousands of New Orleans residents were literally trapped in the Superdome and the Convention Center, waiting for buses from FEMA to slowly arrive and allow them to evacuate, with the last residents being evacuated one week later. Thus, the aftermath of Katrina ignited important, and often uncomfortable, conversations on climate change, disaster risk management, environmental justice, equality, and class.[2] Journalist Vann R. Newkirk compares both Hurricanes Maria and Katrina and asserts that the survivors are living yet today with the lasting effects of flooding, contamination, and ill health, all compounded along lines of race and class.

These hurricanes are devastating, and the underlying reasons that exacerbate their devastation are complex. Most Americans will not have time to research this, or compare and contrast the inequities, nor access a news source that will take the time to do in-depth reporting to educate and raise awareness. Our communities of faith can fill that gap, and need to fill that gap out of a desire to look at the world through a lens of Catholic social teaching. We can inform our faithful about the disparities and be unafraid to wrestle together about the reasons behind the unequal amounts of disaster relief received by citizens of Puerto Rico as compared to citizens of Texas and Florida. Catholic leaders can also help the faithful make comparisons between hurricane victims of Maria and Katrina, hurricanes set twelve years apart but alike in so many ways. Together we can and should grapple with the race and class implications that these hurricanes spotlighted, with the reality of social sin and what our social teachings of the Church have to say when the majority of the victims were brown, black, and/or poor.

---

2. See Vann R. Newkirk II, "The True Scope of the Disaster in Puerto Rico," May 29, 2018, TheAtlantic.com.

As St. Paul worried if he was running the race in vain, the Apostles in Jerusalem responded to him by presenting the key criterion for authenticity: that he should not forget the poor (see Galatians 2:10). Pope Francis builds on this as he reminds that "we may not always be able to reflect adequately the beauty of the Gospel, but there is one sign which we should never lack: the option for those who are least, those whom society discards" (*The Joy of the Gospel*, 195). Many believe that residents of both Puerto Rico and New Orleans were some of the least, too easily discarded by the rest of society.

A destructive force of nature that takes innocent lives becomes much, much worse when human activity impacts and compounds the natural disaster, as in the case of the faulty levees or the inadequate evacuation and disaster relief awarded afterward. The questions haunt us: Were we slow to respond because these human lives somehow had lesser value than other human lives? Were the levees poorly designed, inadequately maintained or tested? Did saving money on maintenance or replacement of levees become more important to a community than the actual lives of the community?

I recognize that it is difficult for our pastors, preachers, and lay leaders who are white, who hold power, or who are in the majority group to initiate or facilitate conversations surrounding the inequalities our brothers and sisters experience today because of their skin color and/or income level, or even mention them. That is true for various reasons. Yet we have a long line of social teachings in the documents and encyclicals of the magisterium to guide and form us to address these questions of class and race, in whatever shape or scenario they present themselves in the modern day. The Church has both a right and obligation to speak.

> The Church's pastors, taking into account the contributions of the different sciences, have the right to offer opinions on all that affects people's lives, since the task of evangelization implies and demands the integral promotion of each human being. It is no longer possible to claim that religion should be restricted to the private sphere and that it exists only to prepare souls for heaven. (*The Joy of the Gospel*, 182)

We must not be afraid to acknowledge the impact of race and class, and to help all the faithful live with more awareness of those who walk this world with the privilege of inclusion and those who struggle daily with marginalization and indifference. Pastors and deacons must say as much in their homily, and do so frequently, especially when leading a community that enjoys and benefits from the privilege of race or class. With a guest speaker or two to either facilitate or give testimony, a parish leader can organize days of retreat and reflection centered around conversations such as these for their faith community. A public lecture could be organized, with someone like journalist Vann R. Newkirk, staff writer at *The Atlantic* specializing in policies affecting disadvantaged or under-resourced communities, or professor Bryan Massingale, a priest of the Archdiocese of Milwaukee and a leading Catholic social ethicist and scholar of racial justice, invited to keynote the lecture.

Stronger storms, such as those explored thus far in this chapter, are but one result of a warming climate. Steeped in scientific evidence, Pope Francis combines science with both faith and a long history of the Church's social thought in his encyclical on the environment, *On Care for Our Common Home*. He states, "Climate change is a global problem with grave implications: environmental, social, economic, political and for the distribution of goods. It represents one of the principal challenges facing humanity in our day" (*On Care for Our Common Home*, 25). No matter our political stripe, our Holy Father is calling urgent attention to the most important issue of our time with his solid and comprehensive encyclical.

The sad truth is that lesser developed countries will bear the brunt of the consequences of climate change while having little responsibility for the causing of it. The impacts will range from rising sea levels, severe drought, and the presence of stronger and more frequent storms. In a sad twist of irony, Francis points out that "developing countries, where the most important reserves of the biosphere are found, continue to fuel the development of richer countries at the cost of their own present and future" (*On Care for our Common Home*, 52). Likewise, the United States bishops urge us to be aware that, regarding climate change, there are differentiated responsibilities. Because countries such as the United States are a main contributor to greenhouse gases and carbon emissions, and also have the necessary resources at their disposal to work toward solutions to slow the effects of human activity on a warming climate, countries such as ours must also bear the brunt of the responsibility to save a planet in peril. In doing so, the bishops state that attention must be given to "the needs of the poor, the weak, and the vulnerable, in a debate often dominated by more powerful interests" (*Global Climate Change: A Plea for Dialogue, Prudence, and the Common Good*).

> The Church has a responsibility towards creation and she must assert this responsibility in the public sphere.
>
> —*Charity in Truth*, 51

Francis projects that when certain resources are depleted, the inevitability of new wars will spring up. In particular, he mentions the scarcity of clean drinking water, and the already increasing tendency to privatize access to this resource. He reminds, "*Access to safe drinkable water is a basic and universal right, since it is essential to human survival. . . .* Our world has a grave social debt towards the poor who lack access to drinking water, because *they are denied the right to a life consistent with their inalienable dignity*" (*On Care for our Common Home*, 30).

Pope Francis pleads, "These situations have caused sister earth, along with all the abandoned of our world, to cry out, pleading that we take another course. Never have we so hurt and mistreated our common home as we have in the last two hundred years" (*On Care for our Common Home*, 53).

Francis teaches the inviolable dignity of each human being: "We must never forget that the planet belongs to all mankind and is meant for all mankind; the mere fact that some people are born in places with fewer resources or less development does not justify the fact that they are living with less dignity" (*The Joy of the Gospel*, 190). This, it seems to me, is a rally cry for all Christians of good will to rise up in action with our own choices that impact the environment, and to initiate conversation and legislative action on how goods and resources are used and distributed to all peoples of our world.

LITURGY AND PRAYER

We know the misery of a disaster most acutely when it strikes in our local area, yet as Christians, we cannot simply overlook the suffering of our sisters and brothers in other places in the world. People whose lives have been upended by an environmental or natural disaster need to lean on the prayers of others. We need to show up for them, accompanying them in prayer and action, both near and far. The following suggestions will help parishes prepare liturgies and prayer services for immediate and long-term needs.

IMMEDIATE RESPONSE

Evening Prayer
Suggested here is a time of prayer for when a disaster has directly affected the local community. If the parish church has been damaged, a community can still gather; shelters, parking lots and fields, and other spaces, too, are sacred spaces where we can pray. Vespers (Evening Prayer) provides the framework and may be led by a layperson, the ordained, or combination of the two. A parish may choose to use the psalmody, readings, and prayer texts that the Church's Liturgy of the Hours prescribes for the day. Or a service with an Evening Prayer structure may be created to reflect specific circumstances.

A parish might need to make a special effort to reach out to those whose homes, businesses, fields, and other property have been lost. We should not assume the usual channels of communication. People directly impacted by the storm, fire, flood waters, or environmental disaster are often displaced from their homes and find themselves staying in shelters, hotels, or the homes of others. There might also be disruptions to utility services and transportation options. As with other crises, *everyone* in a local community is potentially affected and should be welcomed. Consider offering a potluck supper before or after the time of prayer, along with the availability of donated necessities, such as water, food, clothes, toiletries, and basic medical supplies for those who are in need. This is prayer in action, truly accompanying one another in the twists and turns of life's journey.

> The relationship between the Eucharist and the cosmos helps us to see the unity of God's plan and to grasp the profound relationship between creation and the "new creation" inaugurated in the resurrection of Christ, the new Adam. Even now we take part in that new creation by virtue of our Baptism (cf. Col 2:12ff.).
>
> —*Sacrament of Charity*, 51

If there are deaths or serious injuries associated with the disaster, or there are members of the community who are missing or awaiting rescue, the prayer service should be modified to reflect these realities and to remember those who have perished, are recovering, or are in need of rescue.

A simple setting is desirable when so much has been stripped away. The space can be prepared with a cross, crucifix, or an icon of Christ, especially the *Good Shepherd*, candles, and a bowl with charcoals prepared for incense.[3]

The following are suggestions for music, psalmody, and Scripture.

MUSIC AND PSALMODY

- Opening Hymn: "Watch, O Lord" (Haugen); "At Evening" (Green/Haas); or "God of Day and God of Darkness" (Haugen)
- Psalms: "Let My Prayer Rise before You: Psalm 141" (Janco); "Psalm 91: Be with Me" (Haugen); "Psalm 63: My Soul Is Thirsting" (Joncas); or "Psalm 34: The Cry of the Poor" (Foley)
- Canticle of Mary: Holy Is Your Name (Haas)
- Closing Song: "Nada Te Turbe/Nothing Can Trouble" (Taizé Community); "There Is a Balm in Gilead" (African American Spiritual); "We Walk by Faith" (Haugen)

---

3. An Order of Service is provided on page 82.

Canticles and Readings

- Canticle: Ephesians 1:3–10
- Readings: Matthew 6:25–34; Matthew 11:28–30; Luke 8:22–25; or Luke 11:25–28

Preaching Points

At a time when people may feel they have fallen into an abyss of nothingness, stories offer reassurance and insights and invite us to surrender in trust to God, who is the source of all life and gives us all we need. They can make the Scriptures we proclaim even more concrete and relatable. Are there community members who can tell their story of loss through a prism of faith and hope? Alternatively, the presider might find a story to inspire and encourage those gathered. An excellent source for stories is the StoryCorps project: https://storycorps.org.

Intercessions

Here are a few suggestions; the wording should be adapted to fit particular needs.

For the members of our community who have suffered the loss of their homes, businesses, and personal belongings, may they be consoled and supported as they discern next steps, we pray:

For our family members and neighbors who are especially vulnerable—the sick and those with medical needs, the elderly, the very young, those who lack the financial resources needed to seek proper shelter or rebuild—that they find in us a community who will assist and care for them, we pray:

For utility workers, first responders, and the many volunteers who are assisting with providing shelter and food to those displaced from the [*identify disaster*] and who are helping with the cleanup and rebuilding process, may they be safe in their work and know the community's gratitude, we pray:

For the people of [*name the country/area affected*] who are suffering in the wake of [*identify the disaster*], may they find strength in God and support from the global community, we pray:

For this community, may we respond with generosity and compassion to the people of [*name the country/area affected*], we pray:

Sunday Mass

CANTOR ANNOUNCEMENT

The cantor may reference the disaster and invite the assembly to a time of silence. Consider the following hymns for the various parts of the Mass: "I Heard the Voice of Jesus Say" (traditional; various publishers); "The King of Love My Shepherd Is" (traditional; various publishers); "Eye Has Seen" by Marty Haugen (GIA); and "Christ Be Our Light" by Bernadette Farrell (OCP).

PREACHING POINTS

Environmental and natural disasters frequently have widespread and long-term consequences. They can be especially devastating for people who struggle to make ends meet, who are poor, without a home, unemployed, or unable to work. In what ways do the Scriptures call us to lift up the poor and care for our sisters and brothers in need? What actions can we take in the wake of a disaster when we see the disproportionate impact due to the economic advantage of some and the despair of people who are low income or live in poverty? What does the Gospel call us to do to assist people in need here and now and to seek lasting solutions that are in the service of justice?

INTERCESSIONS

Refer to the suggestions on page 42 for disasters that affect the local area. When a disaster strikes people in places unfamiliar to us, we also need to bid the assembly to lift up their needs in prayer. These should be included at Sunday and weekday Masses in an ongoing way.

PREPARATION OF THE GIFTS

If the disaster has impacted the local area, ask parishioners to bring needed items (such as food, personal care items, and clothing) for those in the community who have suffered losses. Representative members of the assembly can then bring forward donated items in the procession with the bread and wine. If the disaster is elsewhere in the country or world, a donation out of the collection can be made to a national or international organization that is assisting those in crisis.

EUCHARISTIC PRAYER

Eucharistic Prayer III is very appropriate for the needs of creation. It is in this text that we hear that God "gives life to all things and makes them holy, . . . / so that from the rising of the sun to its setting a pure sacrifice / may be offered to [his] name." This prayer is extremely appropriate to pray when the needs of creation face us. Even Eucharistic Prayer II, with the comparison of the Holy Spirit to the "dewfall," is appropriate. Use option

II for the Memorial Acclamation, for it is through the ordinary means of bread and wine (the grain and fruit of creation) that we are blessed with the Body and Blood of Christ.

ONGOING PRAYER

As discussed in the ministry section of this chapter, environmental and natural disasters bring to the forefront the long-term, yet urgent, matter of climate change. Being Catholic means having a strong sacramental imagination, one rooted in the sacramentality—the inherent *goodness*—of the created world in which we live. We encounter the sacred in creation; God invites our participation in the ongoing work of creation and charges us with the care of the created world. We use the simple things of the earth—water, fire, grain to make bread, grapes pressed into wine, plants to derive oils—for our sacramental rituals. These simple things of the earth are at risk. How can we, for whom they become extraordinary when we gather for liturgy, not be alarmed and not act as we should as stewards of what God has created?

Perhaps parish communities need to be more intentional about regularly celebrating creation. Doing so will heighten the awareness that creation is a primary source of God's self-revelation and that we need to care for it as an expression of praise and gratitude. A number of resources for communal worship have become available in recent years to encourage faith communities to celebrate and care for creation. See, for example:

- Prayers to Care for Creation from the United States Conference of Catholic Bishops: http://www.usccb.org/prayer-and-worship/prayers-and-devotions/prayers/prayers-to-care-for-creation.cfm
- Prayer Resource from the Catholic Climate Covenant: https://catholicclimatecovenant.org/resources/?tid=15
- Prayer Vigil for the Care of Creation—Taizé Community: https://www.taize.fr/en_article24641.html

Parishes can draw attention to the care of creation by celebrating the annual World Day of Prayer for Creation, on September 1, which would be another opportunity for an ecumenical or interreligious gathering. Other possibilities to celebrate creation include the following:

- **Rogation days** are days of prayer and fasting. Although not officially celebrated in the United States, traditionally they may occur on the three days before Ascension Thursday (Monday, Tuesday, and Wednesday). Since Ascension usually occurs in the spring, these are good days to offer the Blessing of Fields and

Flocks (*Book of Blessings*, chapter 26) and the Order for the Blessing of Seeds at Planting Time (*Book of Blessings*, chapter 27).

- The **Memorial of St. Francis** on October 4 is a wonderful day to have a Blessing of the Animals (*Book of Blessings*, chapter 25).

- The **Memorial of St. Isidore**, the farmer or farm laborer, occurs in the United States on May 15. On this day, offer a blessing of farmers, farm laborers, the land, crops, farm machinery, and so on. You may use and adapt those prayers found in the *Book of Blessings*, chapters 24 (Blessing of Tools or Other Equipment for Work) and 26 (Blessing of Fields and Flocks).

- **Earth Day** takes place on April 22. Although there is no general blessing for the earth, you might adapt what is found in the Order for the Blessing of Fields and Flocks (*Book of Blessings*, chapter 26). Consider also the Masses mentioned below under "Mass."

- On August 15, the **Solemnity of the Assumption of the Blessed Virgin Mary,** there is a long-standing tradition of blessing the first fruits of the harvest for Mary is the first fruit of the Resurrection. This blessing is found in chapter 28 of the *Book of Blessings.*

Other Prayer Options

Besides those days that are date-specific, there are other ways to include the needs of creation on a regular basis in parish prayer.

BLESSINGS

We need to encourage and equip our parishioners to use the blessings found in the *Book of Blessings* or *Catholic Household Blessings and Prayers.* As a community recovers and rebuilds, a parish can turn to these blessings to bless restored or new homes, businesses, fields, animals, buildings, and so on. These blessings remind us that all comes from God. People can celebrate and bless the good things of creation on their own—in their families, with neighbors and friends, and in small groups in the parish. Parish staff can help by making the texts of various blessings available to parishioners and offering guidance on their celebration. It is in our Christian bones to bless and give praise for God's gifts; all that is needed are the blessing texts, water from the baptismal pool, and a little guidance, and the blessings of the Church will take deep root in the way people see the created world.

MASSES

At Sunday and weekday Masses parishes might regularly include in the Universal Prayer an intercession for the care of creation (see above for examples). We hear in the Gospel accounts Jesus' parables and sayings that refer to things of creation. These are ideal texts for a homilist to talk about the sacredness of creation and our responsibilities for sustaining it. These are matters of justice. Many of our hymns also help us to praise God for the wonders of creation and should be included in a parish's repertoire, such as "For the Beauty of the Earth" (traditional; various publishers); "Morning Has Broken" (traditional; various publishers); "Canticle of the Sun" by Marty Haugen (OCP); "We Praise You, O Lord" by Damean Music (GIA); "Joyful, Joyful, We Adore Thee" (traditional; various publishers) "Spirit Blowing through Creation" by Marty Haugen (GIA); "Sing Out, Earth and Skies" by Marty Haugen (GIA).

For Weekday Masses, when appropriate, use the Eucharistic Prayers for Various Needs and Occasions and Reconciliation and celebrate the Masses and Prayers for Various Needs and Occasions related to concerns affecting creation such as:

- At Seedtime (#27)
- After the Harvest (#28)
- In Time of Famine or For Those Suffering Hunger (#33)
- In the Time of Earthquake (#34)
- For Rain (#35)
- For Fine Weather (#36)
- For an End to Storms (#37)

MINISTRY AND OUTREACH

Our response as parish leaders must be to form our communities, as people of faith, with the plight of our planet and what it means to live our comfortable and convenient lives at the expense of the poor. By making no lifestyle change in our consumption habits or the burning of fossil fuels, in the vehicles we drive or the waste we make, we live our lives on the backs of the poor. Pope Francis keenly observes, "People may well have a growing ecological sensitivity but it has not succeeded in changing their harmful habits of consumption, which, rather than decreasing, appear to be growing all the more" (*On Care for Our Common Home*, 55). The increasing use of plastic, the demand for air conditioning, and our resistance to public transportation and renewable energy sources are cause for concern and examples of where we can each vow to make a difference.

> *The Church has a responsibility towards creation* and she must assert this responsibility in the public sphere.
>
> —*Charity in Truth*, 51

When faith communities hear of natural disasters such as hurricanes, tsunamis, wildfires, tornadoes, flooding, disease, or drought, we must respond with compassion, with prayer, with financial donations, with acts of solidarity, and with formation around issues like climate change or racial and economic justice. We must preach a healthy image of God and remind our faithful of a good and loving God, a God who does not strike out in anger or punish a certain population with a disease or illness such as HIV and AIDS, COVID-19, or a heavy-hitting storm. Sadly, there are some who believe and promulgate this, whether consciously or unconsciously, about God, who is all good, all loving, and all merciful.

IMMEDIATE RESPONSE

Here are practical, immediate responses that any faith community can engage in when a natural disaster strikes:

- Encourage participation in a second collection, organizing donations for Catholic Relief Services or where the diocese directs. Emphasize that every dollar matters, and ask that they be as generous as they are able.
- Organize a food drive.
- Be a host site for a blood drive.
- Organize a drive for personal care items: toothpaste, shampoo, deodorant, combs, soap, razors, etc., as well as socks, underwear, bottles, formula, and diapers.
- Consider a toy drive, stuffed animals, or art supplies for children living in temporary housing.
- If you are in a safe area, encourage parishioners to open their home to displaced people seeking shelter (including their pets).
- Partner with local organizations such as Catholic Charities or Red Cross to see if specific things such as cases of water or food for victims or volunteer teams are needed.
- Organize volunteer teams to go to disaster sites in the weeks and months following a natural disaster, remembering that cleanup efforts are messy, slow, and arduous and go on long after the media coverage falls away.
- Ask if the local animal shelters need help fostering pets until animals can be reunited or adopted. Often animal shelters are taking pets from thousands of miles away to relieve the burden at the site of the disaster.

- Send prayers and notes of support to victims of a natural disaster. Gather your faith community after Mass to make cards and write prayers for the well-being of whoever will receive the card.

When the immediate need is met, we can help our communities of faith look at long-term commitments and initiate formation and catechesis around the frequency and growing intensity of the natural disasters we face, especially when they are climate related. Perhaps we challenge our communities to do the following:

- Not buying anything new (clothing, dishes, decorative items, etc.) and consider instead buying used goods only for a certain amount of time
- Lessening the amount of red meat we eat and talking about the cost of sustaining that cow over its lifetime in terms of land and grain
- Pledging to not use any one-time plastic—especially straws, plastic bags, and foam containers—which are not biodegradable and can stay in our landfills for hundreds of years
- Lessening our heating, cooling, and/or electrical use for a period of time (think Lenten fasts as an example) to be in solidarity with our sisters and brothers living in developing nations who have no choice about those things, or those affected by a large-scale natural disaster who also are learning to live without

ONGOING EFFORTS

When there are oil spills in our shared waters—such as when the BP Deepwater Horizon drilling rig exploded off the coast of Louisiana in April 2010 and caused the worst oil spill in US history, dumping 4.9 million barrels of oil into the Gulf of Mexico—we can act as a parish, even if we are not situated anywhere near an ocean. We can donate to clean up efforts and initiate conversation about the use of fossil fuels, perhaps engaging in a parish-wide study of renewable energy forms or studying our own carbon footprint. Children can be encouraged to make an underwater mural depicting the vast diversity of sea life and quotes about the goodness of creation that hangs in a prominent place as we pray for the well-being of our oceans and all the creatures that inhabit it, and strive to realize our interconnectedness to it all.

Shifting our minds to a new kind of disaster, it would be remiss not to draw attention to disease with a brief discussion of the recent Ebola and COVID-19 outbreaks. Between 2014 and 2016, West Africa experienced a rapidly spreading and fatal disease new to most of us: the Ebola Virus

Disease (EVD). Two-and-a-half years after the first case was discovered, the outbreak finally ended. More than 28,600 known cases were confirmed, and at least 11,325 deaths occurred in that time in these nations.

The disease was in the news a lot, but for those of us living far from it, it was hard to imagine the sheer magnitude of what was happening to our sisters and brothers across the globe. What were parish communities to do from far away? Many showed prayer support in the Universal Prayer and on prayer lines. Parish leaders could also seize the opportunity to gather the faithful together to talk about the enormity of this fast-paced disease and alleviate fears that people might have about it as well as build empathy. A disease of this magnitude would be a perfect time to collaborate with the parish nurses or health and wellness committees to educate the community in what the disease was, how it was spreading, and what was being done. Together, faith communities could explore how scary and devastating isolation would be, especially when interacting with health-care workers dressed in biohazard suits while being removed from loved ones and familiar spaces. Perhaps stories of leprosy could be explored in Scripture using the prayer form *lectio divina*, and parallels drawn to this outbreak. Besides praying for victims, perhaps local communities of faith could empower medical teams and help fund research efforts to combat the outbreak. Finally, challenging our communities of faith to embrace St. Paul's exhortation, "Weep with those who weep" (Romans 12:15) is a worthy exercise in empathy and compassion.

At the time of this printing, the coronavirus (COVID-19) pandemic was causing great fear and panic among the global community. This pneumonia-like illness had been detected in more than a million people as it spread like wildfire from country to country; hundreds of thousands and possibly millions (53,000 dead by April 3 , 2020) would lose their lives. World leaders and medical experts grappled with how to control the virus and protect their citizens. By April 3, about four billion people, about half the planet's population, had been placed under some type of order to stay in their homes. In just months, COVID-19 had infected people in 172 nations on six continents. With an increasing number of infections in Central American and African countries in the early spring, concern grew about how healthcare would be provided in developing nations. Though people in Iran heeded the stay-at-home order, with an increasing death toll in the thousands at the beginning of April, the nation closed its parks and gardens to deter people from congregating. At the end of March, India was among the countries that had instituted a lockdown. Parts of China were locked down months beforehand, and Italy had been locked down in stages to prevent the spread and isolate the virus. In the United States, travel bans were put in place, and healthcare workers put themselves at risk to treat those who were ill and quarantined. Makeshift hospitals were established in hotels and conference centers, even in Central Park. Out of fear and increased anxiety, basic supplies and essentials disappeared from store shelves as people bought items in bulk. The empty medicine, pasta, and toilet paper shelves had an eerie feeling. Schools and businesses closed, concerts and political rallies were canceled, college and professional sports were suspended, restaurants and flights sat empty, Disneyland closed, and Broadway and late-night TV went dark. People heard the term "social distancing" frequently and were urged to work from home if possible and curtail social engagements. Most state governments gradually enforced stay-at-home guidelines for weeks as the virus spread and the death toll mounted. The national economy became extremely fragile, with ten million jobs lost by the beginning April as people were unable to work and businesses closed. Worry consumed the global community for their health, safety, and financial stability.

The COVID-19 outbreak affected our elderly the most, especially those living in nursing homes and assisted-living facilities, both in terms of the number affected as well as mortality rates. As with most crises, the poor and the elderly, the homeless and the migrant are most severely impacted. How can you wash your hands frequently or practice social distancing if you live on the streets, sleep in shelters, or are on the move as an undocumented person in search of safety?

Who could have envisioned that during our own lifetime, multiple dioceses—from the Vatican to Seattle—would suspend the celebration of the liturgy for an indefinite period in an effort to help control the virus? That Holy Week would not occur? That Christian initiation would be postponed? That funerals could not be celebrated with family present?

Social media became a source of spiritual communion as Masses (without congregations) were streamed virtually, homilies were filmed and shared, prayer intentions were posted, and communities were strengthened by virtual support. Publishers and communities joined together to provide assemblies with digital resources to pray and connect as the Body of Christ at home. What is clear from this experience is the great need for the Church—all the baptized—to be a constant witness of the peaceful love of Christ. We must always see in each other the face of Christ—in the poor and the powerless, the sick and the scared. We must always look beyond our own needs and give all we can to help our neighbor—beyond our own backyard and borders and among the "friends" we encounter in our real and virtual lives. We must empower the domestic Church to be people of prayer and find ways to gather. We must draw strength from our eucharistic communities of faith and build stronger connections to our source of faith when normalcy returns. We must always be the face of hope to all we encounter.

CONCLUSION

We close this chapter with gratitude to St. Francis of Assisi who, more than anything, taught us to love this planet, and all creatures who dwell on it. To him, each and every creature was a sister or brother united to him, thus urging him to care for all that exists, and to see the divine in it, for each creature bears the indelible mark of its Creator. Pope Francis explains:

> Most High, all-powerful, good Lord,
> yours is the praise,
> the glory and the honor
> and every blessing.
>
> —St. Francis of Assisi, *Canticle of the Creatures*

Such a conviction cannot be written off as naive romanticism, for it affects the choices which determine our behavior. If we approach nature and the environment without this openness to awe and wonder, if we no longer speak the language of fraternity and beauty in our relationship with the world, our attitude will be that of masters, consumers, ruthless exploiters, unable to set limits on their immediate needs. By contrast, if we feel intimately united with all that exists, then sobriety and care will well up spontaneously. (*On Care for Our Common Home*, 11)

Would that a piece of Francis' attitudes and relationship with the created world live within us all!

CHAPTER FOUR

Sudden Deaths
or Accidents

For God so loved the world that he gave his only-begotten Son, so that
everyone who believes in him might have eternal life.

—John 3:16

THEOLOGICAL AND SOCIAL CONTEXT

When the I-35W bridge collapsed in Minneapolis, Minnesota, on August 1, 2007, I remember exactly where I was when I first heard the news. It was one of those moments many Minnesota natives are also able to recall clearly. I was sitting in an auditorium on the campus of St. John's University in Collegeville, Minnesota, with about two hundred other Catholic leaders, listening to a keynote address on the Holy Spirit's call to vocation in lay ecclesial ministry. It was part of a national symposium the School of Theology was sponsoring to help bring to life the USCCB document *Co-Workers in the Vineyard of the Lord*, released two years previously. I recall that his talk was interrupted to make the announcement about the bridge since many in the room were from Minnesota and the campus was just over an hour north of the Twin Cities. A request for prayers was placed before us, and some people got up to check on the safety of loved ones, but the presentation went on. Sitting here, more than a decade later, it seems that perhaps we, the Church, the living Body of Christ, could have and perhaps should have, done more. After all, we had over two hundred lay, religious, and ordained leaders gathered together. Did we fail in a lack of a pastoral response? But it's also true that sometimes we don't realize the enormity, the sheer magnitude, of what we are being faced with in the moment we first hear about something.

It turns out that the collapse happened during rush hour on the third busiest bridge in the state. It was an eight lane bridge that carried vehicles across the St. Anthony Falls of the Mississippi River near downtown Minneapolis. One hundred and eleven vehicles were involved, along with eighteen construction workers who were working on repairs to the bridge. Some vehicles, along with tons of cement and iron, fell and were submerged in the river below, whereas most vehicles were stranded on collapsed sections of the bridge. Cars, semi trucks, and even a school bus carrying sixty-three children returning from a field trip to a local water park could be seen teetering dangerously close to a guard rail on a collapsed section, while a semi truck on fire burned near the bus. This was a big deal; a tragic accident for the city, the state, and the nation. Ninety-three people were rescued in about three hours, thanks to the Minneapolis Fire Department, Minneapolis Police, the state's emergency personnel, first responders, help from neighboring cities, and over five hundred Red Cross workers. The groups were well prepared and had practiced responses and clarified roles in the aftermath of the terrorist attacks in the United States on September 11, 2001. A couple days later, President George W. Bush visited the site while the Minnesota National Guard, the United States Navy divers, the FBI, and other agencies worked around the clock to assess damage and recover bodies. The Salvation Army provided food and drink to workers, and the Minneapolis Police chaplains set up a family assistance center to help people locate family members, pray with them, and provide a calm presence amidst the fear and chaos. The last body was recovered on August 20, about three weeks after the disaster. All in all, thirteen people were dead and one hundred forty five people injured, including twenty-two children. Sitting in the auditorium on the evening of August 1, I couldn't imagine the enormity of the disaster that had just happened in my home state.

Along with the presence of the police chaplains, there were certainly other ministers and religious leaders on hand in those first weeks to provide spiritual support to those in shock or grieving. A makeshift memorial sprung up nearby with signs, photos, and flowers being left by those saddened and wanting to show support. The Minnesota Twins called for a

> In death, Christ calls [humanity] to himself.
>
> —Catechism of the Catholic Church, 1011

moment of silence at the start of the first game in the aftermath, and put up an image behind home plate of the I-35W sign along with the date: 8-1-07 and left it there for the remainder of the season. Interfaith services were organized and held at downtown congregations.

But what about the outlying parishes not in the immediate vicinity of the Twin Cities? How does a tragic accident of this magnitude affect the liturgical and ministerial life of parishes in other cities or rural areas? Certainly hearts are wounded there, too. Perhaps parishioners had friends and relatives in the vicinity of the bridge that night, or who had traveled on that bridge themselves not too long ago. Some of us might be extra jumpy driving over any bridge for a while in the aftermath of the tragedy, with stark images seared in our brains. Certainly, the fragility and the uncertainty of life comes to mind as we all realize we are only walking this day by the sheer grace of God and we begin to grapple with unwelcomed questions of mortality. How quickly life as we know it can be changed or ended! In the parable of the ten virgins, we are reminded about the coming of the Kingdom of heaven, "Therefore, stay awake, for you know neither the day nor the hour" (Matthew 25:13), and can easily apply it to our own deaths.

This chapter, however, is larger in scope than a tragic bridge collapse in an urban area of the Midwest. So many of our cities and communities have had and will continue to have unique and unexpected tragedies befall them. Perhaps there is a gas explosion at a factory and many local community members are hurt or killed. Perhaps a fire breaks out in a school or hospital. Perhaps there is a carbon monoxide leak or food poisoning at the local care center or assisted living facility and many of the community's seniors and elderly have become ill or died from it. Our imagination, and lived experience of the daily news, knows no bounds here. Each situation will be a challenge to a local parish, but each situation requires a response. Pastoral leaders are both encouraged and challenged to do something. Doing nothing is not an option. As Jesus walked among us, he always reached out to those who were suffering to offer healing words and touch, and he always gave instruction and taught the crowds. We can do no less. So we must find ways to bring people together for prayer, for ritual, for conversation, for support, and for formation.

It is also foreseeable that our faith communities will have to deal with the shock of a well-known and beloved person in the community dying suddenly in an auto accident, or from a massive heart attack. It might be the pastor, a staff person, the mayor, the bishop, or everyone's favorite barber or grocer. We can expect our communities to be visibly shaken, and people will be recounting the last time they saw the person: what the interaction was like, what they said or did, and saying they "just can't believe this." That is our cue. That is when a pastoral leader knows that a parish response is required. As the prophet Isaiah proclaimed, "Comfort, give comfort to my people!" (Isaiah 40:1), we are asked to be instruments of healing and hope to those in our midst who are suffering.

LITURGY AND PRAYER

IMMEDIATE RESPONSE

Prayer Service

A challenge for pastoral ministers is to have a prayer service at the ready to respond immediately to people's desire to come together after a sudden death or accident, sometimes within hours of the event. This calls for a simple yet meaningful prayer service that can readily be adapted to fit the particulars of the event and the needs of the community. A simple structure, such as a Liturgy of the Word, is also inviting to *all* who need a space to grieve and a community where they can find consolation, including people from the broader community.[4]

> The people of God accomplish and perfect this continual repentance in many different ways. They share in the sufferings of Christ by enduring their own difficulties, carry out works of mercy and charity, and adopt ever more fully the outlook of the Gospel message.
>
> —*Rite of Penance, 4*

You will need to consider who is in attendance when preparing this service. Who is expected? Will it be a gathering primarily of parishioners? Have people from the broader community—regardless of religious affiliation—been invited? Will family members and friends of the deceased be present? Will young children and youth be present, especially in situations where a child or young person has died? Will any of the rescue workers, first responders, or providers of medical assistance or other care involved with the accident or sudden death be present? Thinking through who might gather will help with decisions about music, Scripture passages to proclaim, reflections to be given, stories to be told, prayer texts to utilize, and other elements that may be introduced in the prayer service.

Add elements to a worship space that are appropriate to the occasion, such as subdued lighting, if possible; a cross, if not already present in the space; the Paschal candle; an icon of Christ, such as the Good Shepherd; a place for candles that, such as in the case of an accident with multiple

---

4. Refer to page 83 for an outline.

fatalities, can be lit by assembly members as the community enters into the prayer; the parish *Book of the Names of the Dead*; and, possibly, photos of the deceased (if the family has given permission).

INTRODUCTORY RITE

Rather than begin immediately with music, offer the Sign of the Cross and a greeting.[5] The prayer leader (ordained or lay) then welcomes those gathered and comments briefly on the event that has brought people together. The recitation of a poem or other words from the Church's spiritual tradition might help the assembly to be more present and serve as an introduction to the service.[6] Whatever is done, the intention is to set the tone of the occasion—that is, to provide people a space to grieve, to honor the dead, to look to Christ and the Church for solace and hope with an invitation to be silent and aware of Christ's presence. For example:

> Let us begin our prayer with a few moments of silence to honor the life of [N.] / the lives of [N. and N.] / those who died in the [*identify the accident*], to pray for the grieving, and to remember that Christ is with us in our sadness.

The service should include music. A good starting point for selecting an opening song would be those that are often used at parish funerals. A few possibilities are "Be Not Afraid" by Bob Dufford, SJ (OCP), "O God, Why Are You Silent" by Marty Haugen (OCP), and "God Will Wipe the Tears" by Stephen Pishner (GIA).

Particularly when several people have died, designated members of the assembly may come forward one by one during the opening song to light a candle for each person who died. This action could also be done during the time of silence before the opening song.

Although this service is not a funeral liturgy, those who prepare this service can look to the *Order of Christian Funerals* for prayer texts. Adapt the Collects included in this ritual book for the occasion. *The Roman Missal* also includes texts for those who died suddenly, accidentally, or violently, and by suicide. There are also texts for particular faith community leaders, including a pope, bishop, priest, deacon, member of a religious community, and individuals who worked in the service of the Gospel.

---

5.   If there is a procession of ministers, process with instrumental music or a chant or song offered by the choir.

6.   For poetry/passages for reflection, see e.g., *A Sourcebook about Christian Death* (Liturgy Training Publications, 1990); *The Art of Losing: Poems of Grief and Healing* by Kevin Young (an anthology of 150 poems) (Bloomsbury, 2013).

LITURGY OF THE WORD

Here again, we can look to the *Order of Christian Funerals*, which includes numerous Scripture passage that could also be used during prayer services in response to sudden or accidental deaths. These readings are also included in the *Lectionary for Mass* in the Masses for the Dead section. Another option is to consult a resource that helps guide families in preparing the Catholic funeral, such as *Eternal Rest in the Lord: Preparing the Liturgy of the Word at Catholic Funerals* published by LTP. Consider the following order:

- First Reading: Old Testament or a non-Gospel New Testament
- Responsorial Psalm (sung): Psalm 23 (The Lord Is My Shepherd), Psalm 27 (The Lord Is My Light), Psalm 103 (The Lord Is Kind and Merciful)
- Gospel

The preacher might consult a resource on funeral homilies, such as *Funeral Homilies* by William J. Bausch (Twenty-Third Publications, 2009), for talking points concerning Christian perspectives on death. In the case of an accident that has affected the local community, there might be words of encouragement and inspiration offered from local faith and civic leaders. Using poetry and words from the spiritual tradition can be poignant and memorable for people. Clearly, it will be important to acknowledge the bewilderment and sorrow of the community, to express gratitude for the gifts shared by the person or people who have died, and to point to the Paschal Mystery of Jesus Christ as the basis of our hope. In the case of a death by suicide or drug overdose, sensitivity to the family and friends is key, as is the recognition that only God knows the depths of the human heart and of the suffering the deceased experienced in life. None of this is ours to judge.

After the homily, it might be desirable to invite others who knew the deceased to offer words of remembrance. An open-ended invitation works best with a small gathering. If the gathering is large, arranging ahead of time for a couple people to make brief comments is advisable. Good pastoral judgment is needed here to ensure that providing this opportunity is appropriate and adds meaning to the experience and does not create a situation in which people use the time to lay blame or disparage the deceased or others.

Alternatively, the prayer leader might offer a very brief reflection and then invite the assembly to a time of meditation accompanied by music (instrumental, solo, or choir piece). Good musical options include "Shepherd Me, O God" by Marty Haugen (GIA), "What Wondrous Love Is This?"

(traditional; various publishers), or "Precious Lord, Take My Hand" (traditional; various publishers).

A community might inscribe the names of the dead in the parish *Book of the Names of the Dead*. Representative members of the deceased's family or others from the assembly can be invited forward after the reflection, perhaps during a song of meditation or in silence, to write the names in the book.

For inspiration in composing intercessions, we can look to the *Order of Christian Funerals* and other sources of model intercessions such as *Eternal Rest in the Lord: Preparing the Liturgy of the Word at Catholic Funerals*. Here are a few suggestions for wording:

Accidents

For [*names, if known*]/For those who died in [*identify accident*], may God welcome them into the fullness of peace, we pray:

For the families of the deceased and all who are grieving, may they be comforted and strengthened during this painful time, we pray:

For the injured and other survivors, may they be encouraged and cared for as they heal, we pray:

In gratitude for the first responders and others who provided aid and comfort to the individuals involved in [*identify the accident*], may they be safe and supported in their work, we pray:

For those who feel responsible and are burdened with guilt over [*identify the accident*], may they be met with compassion and forgiveness, we pray:

Death of a Local Leader/Community Member

For [*name of person who died*], may our [*brother/sister*] be embraced in Eternal Love, we pray:

For this community, may we be comforted in our grief and strengthened during this time of change, we pray:

Death from Suicide

For [*name of person who died*], may God who knows the human heart and is merciful give peace to our [*brother/sister*], we pray:

For individuals who struggle with mental illness or feel trapped in despair, may the community that surrounds them extend love, understanding, and care, we pray:

For this community, may we be a place of welcome, listening, and support for all who find life difficult, we pray:

Death as the Result of an Overdose

> For [*name of the person who died*] and the members of our community whose lives have been lost to opioids or other drugs, may the Love that awaits welcome them into a place of happiness and peace, we pray:

> For parents, spouses, and children whose loved ones battle addictions, may they find courage in Christ and support in his Church, we pray:

The Lord's Prayer serves as the conclusion to the intercessions. Here is an example of how to introduce this prayer:

> The Lord knows our grief and strengthens us in our sorrow; let us pray as Christ taught us.

CONCLUDING RITE

The service concludes with a closing prayer. As with the opening prayer, we can look to the *Order of Christian Funerals* and *The Roman Missal* (in the Masses for the Dead section) for prayers to adapted to fit the particular circumstances. Offer the final blessing looking to the *Order of Christian Funerals* for options (look to the conclusions of each of the rites found in this ritual book). You might also use: "May God comfort us in our grief and sustain us in the coming days." End with a closing song, or it might be more appropriate for the assembly to depart in silence. When selecting music, look to the parish funeral repertoire for options. A few familiar options are "Blest Are They" by David Haas (GIA), "On Eagle's Wings" by J. Michael Joncas (various publishers), or "We Shall Rise Again" by Jeremy Young (GIA).

Ecumenical or Interreligious Gatherings

Depending on the make-up of the local community and the circumstances, a time of grieving and reflection shared with other Christians and people of other religious traditions may be desirable and could affirm and foster relationships with one another. In the case of an accident, a candlelight procession to the site or other suitable location and/or vigil is easy to organize. Passages from sacred texts or other Scripture readings can be proclaimed; flowers or stones or other symbols to honor the dead can be left at the place. It can be a powerful and memorable experience of solidarity to allow those who are grieving to stand in silent reflection with one another.

When local community leaders have died, or when the community is shaken to the core by a death from suicide or an overdose, people of all religious traditions can gather in a common place for ritual. This could be at one of the churches, synagogues, mosques, or other sacred space, or perhaps at a community place like a park or town square. Again, this might include readings from sacred texts, words of reflection offered by faith leaders, and gestures that honor the individual who has died and that speak to the grieving. All of this, of course, necessitates close collaboration with the local faith leaders.

Sunday Mass

CANTOR'S INTRODUCTION

When welcoming the assembly and announcing the opening hymn, the cantor may include a reference to the sudden death or accident and invite the assembly to a time of silence before the song begins.

PREACHING POINTS

Draw upon the wisdom and experiences of the community. What stories have they shared? How are they as people of faith speaking about the sudden death/accident? Every Sunday is a celebration of the Paschal Mystery. Where are the seeds of resurrection and new life in the sudden death or loss of many lives? Where might the community look—in the faces of the grief-stricken, in the care and comfort of others, in the healing that is assured through our faith in Christ's triumph over death and the promise of eternal life?

INTERCESSIONS

The *General Instruction of the Roman Missal* requires that a petition be written for the local community (see 69–71). This is also a time to remember those whose death was sudden and shocked the community or those who died in a catastrophic accident, as well as the people who are mourning and all who provided assistance and support. The suggestions provided in this resource also work well at Mass.

MUSIC

An instrumental or choir piece during the Preparation of the Gifts or after Communion will invite the assembly to a place of needed contemplation in the wake of the recent tragedy, without overwhelming them or overtaking the liturgy itself.

ONGOING PRAYER

All Saints and All Souls' Day

The community will need time to remember in an ongoing way those who have died. The Solemnity of All Saints and the Commemoration of the Faithful Departed are opportunities to remember those who have died suddenly, as the result of suicide or overdose, or in an accident that impacted the community, alongside other faithful departed who have died in the past year. At Mass, individual names may be mentioned or a reference to the accident that claimed the lives of many may be included in the intercessions. A parish might want to consider an Evening Prayer for the Commemoration of the Faithful Departed and provide space for members of the community to tell stories and share remembrances. In addition, the names inscribed in the *Book of the Names of the Dead* could be read aloud by community members during Evening Prayer. Parish leaders may look to the Office for the Dead for a possible structure for prayer.

Anniversary Dates

Especially in the case of an accident, the anniversary date will be a significant moment. A prayer service like the one outlined above or an Evening Prayer[7] (especially from the Office for the Dead) would be appropriate; at the very least the event could be remembered in the intercessions at a Sunday Mass near the anniversary date. For how many anniversaries should this be done? Listen to the community. Remember that grief is a process. When preparing these Masses, look to the Masses for the Dead in *The Roman Missal*. Prayers are provided for the particular situation or death.

MINISTRY AND OUTREACH

IMMEDIATE RESPONSE

In times like this, it is wise to have listening ministers immediately available for those who need to talk. Stories of shock, grief, loss, fear, and even anger, along with thoughts and feelings surrounding death, will surface. This can be offered by those trained for active listening with ministries such as BeFrienders or Stephens Ministry, along with spiritual directors and parish pastoral staff. These groups and ministers will help those who would like to talk about their feelings and memories, their sadness, fear, or even guilt surrounding the deceased. Time could be provided after weekend Masses as well as on the evening of the tragedy. The pastoral team or grief ministers of the parish offer a ritual: perhaps a large jar and paper hearts are available where people can write a memory, a note, or a prayer that is then given to the family from the faith community.

> When a member of Christ's Body dies, the faithful are called to a ministry of consolation to those who have suffered the loss of one whom they love.
>
> —*Order of Christian Funerals*, 8

---

7. An outline of Evening Prayer is provided on page 82.

Safety permitting, perhaps a march to the place of an accident or death, or gathering there for a candlelight vigil and ritual can be swiftly organized as an ecumenical or interfaith effort by faith communities city-wide within the first week of the tragedy. Flowers and religious symbols could be left at the foot of the bridge, a gong could be tolled for each life lost, songs of hope sung, and feathers released over the water for all of the victims as a symbol of how we are enfolded in God's loving arms and caressed amidst our suffering.

ONGOING EFFORTS

In the long term, catechetical leaders and pastoral ministers may choose to organize a speaker or a workshop centered around becoming more comfortable with death and beginning to be prepared for the inevitability of death. It could focus on healthcare directives, guardianship, wills and estates, or even conversations about how people come to believe in the Church's teaching on the resurrection, salvation, purgatory, and images of the afterlife, and where they struggle or have doubts with the doctrine. I have had many fascinating conversations with people who have beautiful images of what heaven will be like as well as faithful Catholics who struggle with the teachings on purgatory. Let God's people question, doubt, and wrestle! Do not fear conversations like this or insist on strict orthodoxy. Certainly provide the Church's teaching, but also allow room for doubts, questions, and new images that might arise in the adults we serve. People need to wrestle with their faith. It is a sign of a well-formed, maturing faith and points to someone who is advancing in the various stages of faith development as described by James Fowler.[8] Finally, we have to admit that we are, after all, limited in what we know about what will happen to us after death. Even from a faith lens, we are all simply conjecturing about what's next based on what we know and believe about a God who is all good, all loving, and all merciful. Parish ministers might consider offering a program or workshop about self-care amidst grief and loss, or starting a support group for anyone navigating life in the midst of great loss if there isn't one already underway.

Perhaps, a few weeks down the road, people will be given the time and space to dream, envision, talk, and pray about what they hope the next leader (pastor, staff member, bishop, or mayor) will be like and what the community most needs in the next person that the Holy Spirit will tap. This exercise could be very effective when a pope dies (or resigns, as in the case of

---

8. See James W. Fowler, *Stages of Faith: The Psychology of Human Development and the Quest for Meaning* (New York: HarperCollins), 1981.

Benedict XVI). Giving space for people to prayerfully reflect on the gifts we most hope for, want, and need in our next pontiff, and sharing those with each other, is beneficial. Certainly the parish community coming together to watch the funeral, and the election of the next pope at a conclave, can be powerful, unifying experiences.

Special care must be given to those communities who are faced with someone who dies by suicide. Suicide is a great tragedy. When we learn the depths of someone's pain and anguish, when we realize that the thought of death was preferable to the hell they were living, when we know of the mental illness or the addiction that may have accompanied the decision to commit suicide, we are all shaken. The entire Body of Christ weeps and suffers for the pain this person experienced, for those left behind, and for the irrevocability of the act itself.

Suicide

Suicide leaves an awful wake in its destructive path. Young people might be tempted to imitate the act when they see the attention it gets, causing a community to experience multiple deaths by suicide. So many family members and friends say they never knew, or never saw signs, of the pain someone is in. Survivors are left with huge burdens of guilt to wade through, unpack, and eventually leave at the cross. The community of faith has to be there offering physical and spiritual support to help them do that.

The Catholic Church proclaims that human life is sacred and that every person is precious. This is the first and foundational principle at the heart of our Catholic social tradition. The *Catechism of the Catholic Church* offers strong words on the sanctity of human life and honoring the Creator by fully living the life we've been given (paragraph 2280):

> Everyone is responsible for his life before God who has given it to him. It is God who remains the sovereign Master of life. We are obliged to accept life gratefully and preserve it for his honor and the salvation of our souls. We are stewards, not owners, of the life God has entrusted to us. It is not ours to dispose of.

Yet we must equally proclaim that God's mercy prevails in all situations, and the Church welcomes funerals for loved ones who have died by suicide. Many of the faithful today still believe that a loved one is not allowed a church burial and that all hope of salvation is lost. We must proactively speak, preach, and teach to correct that misconception. Three years prior to his papacy, Cardinal Jorge Bergoglio reflected:

> There was a time [when the Church wouldn't] do funerals for suicides, because [the person] didn't keep walking toward the goal; he put an end to

the path when he felt like it. But this is a person who couldn't overcome the contradictions. I don't reject him. I leave it in God's hands.[9]

Pope Francis, in imitation of Jesus Christ, always lands on the side of mercy. He expects pastoral leaders to do the same.

Opioid Epidemic

A final issue deserving mention in this chapter, and a sad sign of the current times, is the opioid epidemic. Too many of our families will experience the death of a family member or friend from a drug overdose. Whether the drug is used on occasion recreationally, or if the drug is part of a pattern of addiction, or if the drug was first used as a painkiller, too many overdoses are occurring everyday in both urban and rural areas. No community is exempt from the presence, lure, and power of drugs. Our families are in crisis. We must educate our parishioners about drug abuse recognition, prevention, and treatment. You must consider inviting a person or family who has dealt with drug addiction or overdose to speak at Catholic high schools, religious education, or at an intergenerational parish event.

Families and individuals who are facing the death of loved ones as a result of drug addiction face unique grief. These survivors often have feelings of guilt, they may worry about the state of the loved one's soul due to perceived sin of addiction, and they often experience grief shrouded in intense shame. Lay and ordained ministers should be aware of the long-term trauma such families may have endured as they grieve the death of a person who may have become unrecognizable to them in recent months, or help them face the shock of a death of a person who they were unaware suffered addiction to illegal drugs. When praying with survivors, recognize the trauma that they or their loved ones have endured. Meet them in their grief. Educated ministers can meet survivors and help them when they are deeply mired in grief. In such ministry, we can be the hands and feet of Jesus.

Formational work can be done by pastoral leaders on the role of suffering in the life of Christ, and in our own lives. Like many of you, I would prefer never to feel physical pain, and I am quick to grab an aspirin for a headache or achy joints. This expectation that we will sail through life without feeling pain, especially after injuries or surgeries, is not realistic. Yet it's prevalent. What can we learn from suffering? Does pain have anything to teach us? What happens to our faith when we are faced with severe acute pain or wake up facing daily chronic pain? Can the pain one knows in daily life somehow unite him or her with the anguish our God knew in the betrayal

---

9. *Pope Francis: In His Own Words* (Novato, CA: New World Library, 2013), 79.

and crucifixion? The questions are worthy ones to ponder in prayer or through journaling.

Another way to engage a wide audience with the topic of opioids is to invite a moral theologian in to have the community wrestle with these questions: Are addictions a result of sin or sickness? If there is sin involved, is it personal or social? If it is social sin, how culpable is our whole society? Offerings like these raise awareness and get people talking about the issue that our communities are facing. Any and all pastoral initiatives surrounding this issue are truly a response of mercy.

CONCLUSION

Grief is a process. We heal in layers and over time. In the immediate aftermath of the sudden death of a familiar member of our local community or an accident that claims the lives of people known or unknown to us, we are overwhelmed with shock and sadness. It is hard to know what to think or feel or even what to bring to prayer, how to act, and how to minister to others. Yet people instinctively want to come together close in time to the event to grieve, to honor the dead, to try to make sense of what happened. As the grieving process unfolds, we also need to find ways to remember those who have died beyond the actual time of their death and we need to continue healing, both individually and as a community, as we gather for Sunday worship and other times of prayer and allow the circumstances to shape our ministry at these times.

Come to me, all you who labor and are burdened, and I will give you rest. Take my yoke upon you and learn from me, for I am meek and humble of heart; and you will find rest for yourselves. For my yoke is easy, and my burden light.

—Matthew 11:28-30

CHAPTER FIVE

Local Situations

*As a body is one though it has many parts, and all the parts of the body,
though many, are one body, so also Christ.*

*If one part suffers, all the parts suffer with it; if one part is honored,
all the parts share its joy.*

—1 Corinthians 12:12, 26

THEOLOGICAL AND SOCIAL CONTEXT

I have been in leadership positions on parish staffs as a big change was brewing—in one case, in a strong, independent, vibrant city parish committed to both campus ministry and the social teachings of the Church. This parish was asked to cluster with two other neighboring parishes and go from having its own full-time pastor to sharing two priests among three parishes. The model we had to use in the diocese was that of a rural area that had clustered five small parishes being served by two priests, but now clustering had moved into the city and was affecting large urban parishes as well. It was an incredibly difficult process to accompany a parish community through this change.

I have also served on a parish staff in a rural area that made the extremely difficult decision to close its Catholic school. After decades of thriving and providing excellent Catholic education to multiple generations, the parish leaders recognized that the vastly diminished class size was detrimental to both student life and parish life, and after years of discussion they made the difficult decision to move the community toward closure.

The planning for changes of this magnitude was both intense and intentional, and the loss experienced by each community was real. The vast spectrum of emotions displayed by parishioners ranged from sadness to anger and, for some, a decision to walk away from their parish community. The emotions did not quickly dissipate, either, but rather lived within the community for years. I witnessed that anger and frustration over decisions such as these can fester and act like poison in parish life.

In addition to school closures and parish clustering, there are also parish closures, parish mergers, parish twinning, and school mergers happening all over the nation as dioceses struggle with dwindling numbers of families investing in Catholic education as well as the staffing realities of a diminishing number of priests available to serve both the parish life and sacramental life. Whatever the situation, whether rural or urban, the decisions are not easy, and the impact felt by the community will be painful.

> In hopeless situations of pain and suffering, God never abandons his children but rather remains close to them.
>
> —Pope Francis

Beyond the clustering and closures, another issue affecting our local communities is the enormity of the sexual abuse crisis. So many of us personally know victims or perpetrators, or sadly, both. After the *Boston Globe* broke the story in early 2002 it became apparent that the problem of Catholic clergy sexually abusing minors was much larger than the Archdiocese of Boston but was, in fact, widespread throughout the United States. As more victims came forward, more allegations became known, in dizzying numbers. It soon became not just a national scandal, but a global crisis for the Catholic Church. There was a culture of abuse for decades in our priests that made it acceptable, maybe even expected, to prey on children.

A major factor at play in this scandal is not just the priests who have abused children, but also the subsequent cover up by the bishops who knew about the crimes being committed and kept them secret by moving the priests around to different locations, allowing them to harm an even greater number of children. This kind of horror has brought our Church to her knees, begging God for mercy. We must repent and have a true *metanoia*, or true conversion of heart. Some are not sure we have reached that point yet, although the faithful are all wide awake and taking every precaution possible to protect our children. Some are disappointed that the Church has not acted more swiftly or strongly with those who have inflicted the abuse and with those who have covered up the situation.

When speaking about the Word of God in a homily on April 13, 2006, Pope Francis stated, "The Word of God always offers a choice: convert and ask for help and more light, or close and cling even more tightly to your chains and darkness." Although he was not referencing the sexual abuse crisis, the pope's words are so very appropriate. We must ask for more help and more light as we forge a new path forward, a new way of being Church. From the words of the prophet Isaiah, "House of Jacob, come, / let us walk in the light of the LORD!" (2:5).

LITURGY AND PRAYER

Rituals, including the Church's liturgy, help us traverse chaos. As parish and diocesan communities grapple with the disgrace of sexual abuse in our Church, we need rituals to lament, atone, and heal, and to experience an authentic and profound transformation of our life together as the Body of Christ. So, too, when communities are touched by the phenomenon of parish and school closings. Rituals are needed to negotiate the gamut of reactions and the experiences of leave-taking, displacement, and formation of new consolidated communities.

Negotiating chaos rarely proceeds in a predictable, logical fashion. Previously unknown abuse cases and incidents of cover-up might surface along the way; unhealed wounds might remain or be reopened; financial constraints or bankruptcies of dioceses might upend plans for building a needed new church for a consolidated community.

Moreover, the abuse scandal and parish closures touch people in different ways. Victims and survivors of abuse and their families have been betrayed in unspeakable ways and at a level more acute than community members who, while deeply troubled and angry, do not have firsthand experiences of abuse. Parishioners whose beloved church or school will be closed can be expected to feel disheartened and adrift as they anticipate a "merger," while communities that prepare to be clustered worry about how their pastoral and spiritual needs will be met. Given this, we need to consider an assortment of ritual experiences that can speak to who and where people are and that invite participants to be open to the healing and transformative power of God's faithfulness and love.

> In the Eucharist the sacrifice of Christ becomes also the sacrifice of the members of his Body. The lives of the faithful, their praise, sufferings, prayer and work, are united with those of Christ and with his total offering, and so acquire a new value.
>
> —*Catechism of the Catholic Church*, 1368

IMMEDIATE RESPONSE

Liturgy of Lament

Lament is one form of prayer that comes most immediately to mind when considering how we might respond with ritual prayer to the tragedy of the sexual abuse of children and youth and to the upset of parish closures and reconfigurations. A Liturgy of Lament will likely be a new experience for most Catholics, but in these times it is what is needed. Advocating for the practice of lament as a means to reform the Church during this time of the abuse scandal, Henry L. Novello points to lament as "the prayer of 'a bruised faith, a longing faith, a faith emptied of nearness.'"[1] Lament can lead us through times of suffering to deeper trust and a renewed hope for a revitalized Church, as we boldly insist that God hear our complaints, our pleas and act as God has promised.

If the liturgy is in response to the abuse scandal, will victims, survivors, and their families be present? If they are, how might they be involved with the movements of the liturgy, such as proclaiming readings or prayer texts, leading song, perhaps witnessing to their experience? Who will lead the time of prayer? A lay leader of prayer? An ordained leader? A combination? If the Liturgy of Lament is in response to a school or parish closing, a decision to merge or cluster parishes, the assembly may include puzzled students and parents, teachers and other school staff facing job loss, concerned individuals from the local neighborhood, parishioners and staff from both the parish to be closed and the other parish that will form a new consolidated community. How might these various generations of stakeholders be drawn into the ritual experience?

A Liturgy of Lament calls for simplicity of space and a sober yet always hopeful tone. Dimmed lighting and a single candle may be appropriate, and a cross or crucifix, or icon of Christ—for example, an icon of Christ with children or an icon of the Holy Trinity. In the case of a parish or school closing, an icon, painting, or sculpture of the community's patron saint might be added, as well as a few items of historical significance that are recognizable and meaningful to the assembly. Also consider the use of incense.

One approach for a Liturgy of Lament would be to follow an order of service for Evening Prayer[2] and utilize psalms of lament.[3] Another would

---

1. Henry L. Novello, "The Sexual Abuse of Minors in the Church: Reform through the Practice of Lament," *Worship* 92 (May 2018): 230, citing Kathleen D. Billman and Daniel L. Migliore, *Rachel's Cry: Prayer of Lament and Rebirth of Hope*, (Eugene, OR: Wipf and Stock, 1999), 124. Novello's article helps one appreciate the biblical tradition of lament and how we can draw upon this tradition in shaping a Christian prayer of lament.

2. An outline for Evening Prayer is found on page 82.

3. For suggestions on communal experiences of lament, see J. Frank Henderson, *Liturgies of Lament* (Chicago: Liturgy Training Publications, 1994). While this resource does not include a liturgy specific

be to create a ritual of lament influenced by the pattern of a psalm of lament, as noted below[4]:

- Address to God
- Complaint or lament
- Confession of trust
- Petition for help
- Words of assurance
- Vow of praise[5]
- [Sending]

ADDRESS TO GOD

After beginning with the Sign of the Cross and a greeting, on behalf of those gathered, the presider addresses God. Here are some examples of texts based on need.

Sexual Abuse

We cry out to you, O God, hear us! Countless lives have been shattered by the sins of priests and bishops who betrayed your people. Predators have violated our children. Grief torments parents. Painful memories of abuse haunt women and men. Shameful actions by those entrusted to lead have brought shame and suffering to our Church. How long, O God, must your people endure this disgrace?

Parish or School Closure, Merger, or Clustering

O God, attend to our anguish. Our hearts are bitter. We know only disappointment and fear. Will change fracture our parish community? Will we be forever displaced?

Silence may follow the address. You might consider accompanying the silence with somber instrumental music or an opening song sung by all following a period of extended silence. Some suggestions: "Psalm 22: My God, My God," or "O God, Why Are You So Silent?" both by Marty Haugen (GIA) or "Wait for the Lord" (Taizé Community/GIA).

---

to the sexual abuse scandal or parish closings, the included outlines of liturgies can be adapted. The book also includes lists of scripture readings and psalms, prayers, and other liturgical texts. This resource is out of print, but copies are still available from used-book sellers. See also J. Frank Henderson, "Abuse of Children: A Liturgy of Lament," Rite (October 2002): 10–12; Michael Weldon, *A Struggle for Holy Ground: Reconciliation and the Rites of Parish Closure* (Collegeville, MN: Liturgical Press, 2004), 231–235.

4. See Novello, 237–238. Novello's proposed structure includes originally composed prayer texts. I am suggesting here that one rely primarily on psalms to express the community's sentiment.

5. *Liturgies of Lament*, 17.

COMPLAINT OR LAMENT

Select a Responsorial Psalm that expresses the rawness of the community's devastation. The presider or cantor may proclaim or chant the first stanza; the assembly continues, alternating sides. Consider Psalms 9, 13, 22, 42, 43, 54, 55, 69, 77, 83, 88, or 90. Follow the psalm with another period of silence.

CONFESSION OF TRUST

Select a psalm that communicates trust in God. The assembly proclaims or chants the psalm, alternating sides. Alternatively, the psalm is sung responsorially with the cantor leading the assembly. Consider Psalms 25, 27, 31, 56, 57, 59, 63, 70, 71, 85, 86, 89, 95, or 107. Again, follow the psalm with a period of silence.

PETITION FOR HELP

Sing a psalm that is a cry for God's help. It may be proclaimed by one or two voices or be sung by the assembly. Consider Psalms 121 or 130. Follow the psalm with a period of silence.

ASSURANCE

Choose a Scripture reading that reassures the assembly of God's faithfulness, such as Deuteronomy 31:7–8, Joshua 1:1–9, Isaiah 41:17–20, Isaiah 43:1–7, 2 Corinthians 4:1–18 or Philippians 4:4–9. The reading is followed by a period of silence.

PRAISE

Sing a psalm or canticle that expresses praise of God such as Psalms 145 or 146 or the Canticle of Mary.

SENDING

Representative members of the assembly may come forward to the single candle to light tapers; they share the light with the assembly. Once everyone is holding a lit taper, all recess from the worship space, carrying the light into the darkness of the evening. This can be done in silence or to song, such as "Sing a New Church" by Dolores Dufner, OSB (OCP), "We are Marching/*Siyahamba*,"a South American spiritual adapted by David Haas (OCP) or "*Bambelela*/Never Give Up" by Marty Haugen (GIA). The presider concludes with the Sign of the Cross and a dismissal.

Sunday Mass

INTRODUCTION

The priest should address these issues at Sunday Mass. Here are a few examples of introductions to the Mass, based on need:

Sexual Abuse

We gather in solidarity with the children and adults who have suffered at the hands of abusers in our Church. We are people devastated by the failure of Church leaders to be truthful and to do what is right. We are mindful too of our own missteps and need for forgiveness. [*The presider allows for a moment of silence and then introduces the Penitential Act with the proper text from the Missal.*]

Parish or School Closer, Merger, or Clustering

We gather today with heavy hearts. [*Presider should note the situation.*] Let us turn to the Lord in our distress. [*The presider allows for a moment of silence and then introduces the Penitential Act with the proper text from the Missal.*]

PENITENTIAL ACT

The invocations for form III of the Penitential Act can be shaped to speak to what lies heavy on the community's mind and heart. Parish leaders may also compose new prayers so long as they follow the form and structure of the prayers found in the Missal. Here are some examples:

Sexual Abuse

Lord Jesus, you hear the cries of those who have been sexually violated and deceived by clergy and religious in our Church. Lord, have mercy.

Christ Jesus, you know our suffering and bind our wounds. Christ, have mercy.

Lord Jesus, you love the victims and survivors of abuse and strengthen us to embrace and comfort them. Christ, have mercy.

Parish or School Closure, Merger or Clustering

Lord Jesus, you free us from the disappointment that may close us off to the new life promised. Lord, have mercy.

Christ Jesus, you transform any bitterness in our hearts and bring us peace. Christ, have mercy.

Lord Jesus, you nourish us with your Body and Blood so we may carry out our mission as Church in the world. Lord, have mercy.

PREACHING POINTS

Most needed in these times is radical honesty. People feel deceived by the sexual abuse scandal and often enough by decisions to close, merge, or cluster their beloved parishes or schools. How important it is to listen to people—to their stories of anguish and hurt, of confusion and anxiety, but also to their stories of faith and hope and love for the Church. Yes, even in the midst of deeply disturbing events, they *love* the Church, which they and all of the baptized are. We need to rally the baptized to *be even more* the Church that they are because of their shared life in Christ. And all of us need to be reassured during these difficult times that God suffers with us and will never abandon us or the Church that God called into being.

ONGOING PRAYER

Communal Lament

The suggestion for a Liturgy of Lament as a more immediate response does not preclude the use of communal lament as a community works through this difficult time, whether in their local parish or diocese or in the universal Church. In other words, a periodic Liturgy of Lament may be appropriate. As the community continues to come to terms with this scandal, a ritual of atonement or penitential service might be appropriate. A good resource for these services are the nonsacramental penance services in the *Rite of Penance*, which may be adapted for particular needs. Later, a healing service or prayer for the renewal of the Church may be desirable. As mentioned, there is not a predictable order of things here. We need to listen to the community.

Going forward, it will be important to celebrate the diversity of people and gifts in the newly consolidated or clustered community. We might look to the *Book of Blessings* for inspiration. There are blessings for students and teachers (which can be expanded to include all staff[6]), those who exercise pastoral service (such as parish staff, catechists, other volunteers[7]), who have particular liturgical roles, who serve on parish council, and who are involved with other parish groups.[8] Aspects of the community that may be new or enhanced—for example, more racial and cultural diversity, more languages spoken, more persons with differing abilities—will shape future liturgies. How will a potentially more diverse assembly celebrate liturgy differently? Consider the hospitality of the space and community, the style of liturgical music, the worship environment, the preaching and prayer texts, the language(s) of the celebration, the ritual actions, and who serves in particular liturgical roles that support the assembly's worship.

---

6. See chapter 5 in the *Book of Blessings*.
7. See chapter 60 in the *Book of Blessings*.
8. See chapters 61-65 in the *Book of Blessings*.

Liturgy and Ministry in Times of Need

MINISTRY AND OUTREACH

It is important to over-communicate to the parish community when considering large scale changes to the structure of a parish or school. Too often a message is said in the homily or announcements, or printed in the bulletin or newsletter, and it is assumed that people are then in the know. The reality is that the message needs to be communicated repeatedly, by various means, to ensure that the majority of people actually hear it and internalize it. It's also important to allow people input into the decisions at hand. This means real input, not just holding a parish meeting where people believe they have a say, but in reality the decision has already been made and parish leadership is just going through the motions. If the decision has already been made, it's important to tell people that up front.

Resources

In the matter of parish or school closures, mergers, and clustering of parishes, there will be stages to the transition—from initial announcement to celebrating the history of a community and its sacred spaces to leave-taking to forming a consolidated community, and eventually celebrating a community's new life and mission. There are helpful resources to turn to, since unfortunately, we are becoming more experienced with these occasions. First, contact the diocesan worship office for guidance on rituals to mark the various stages of a parish or school closing or merger/clustering. Michael Weldon's excellent book *A Struggle for Holy Ground: Reconciliation and the Rites of Parish Closure* (Liturgical Press, 2004) offers suggestions for a series of rituals to help a community negotiate the trauma of a parish closure, including a Ritual of Group Grieving, a Reconciliation Rite for Impasse, Rituals of Transition: A Week of Farewell for Parish Closure, and Rites for the Inauguration of a Newly Consolidated Parish, among others. A rite for the closing of a church is also included in Thomas G. Simons' *Holy People, Holy Place: Rites for the Church's House* (Liturgy Training Publications, 1998).[9] Also see Kevin Mannara's *That All May Be One: Consolidating Church Buildings When Parishes Merge*

> All of you who feel heavily the weight of the cross, you who are poor and abandoned, you who weep, you who are persecuted for justice, you who are ignored, you the unknown victims of suffering, take courage. You are the preferred children of the kingdom of God, the kingdom of hope, happiness and life. You are the brothers of the suffering Christ, and with Him, if you wish, you are saving the world.
>
> —Address of Pope Paul VI to the Poor, the Sick, and the Suffering (December 8, 1965)

9. A revised, second edition will be available in 2021.

(Liturgy Training Publications, 2015) for recommendations on transforming a common worship space.

It is wise to continue to offer listening sessions and listening ministers for people who feel saddened or angered by the changes taking place in the faith community they have known and loved. Don't expect people to "get over it" too quickly because like any loss, grief is personal and looks different for each individual. Consider inviting in grief counselors to talk about strategies for dealing with loss, and how to work through grief.

Community Changes

The most important thing parish leadership can do with large-scale changes affecting a local community is to be transparent and honest. Be forthcoming in the amount of information offered up front, and answer any and all questions as completely and thoroughly as possible. Do not hide or withhold information, even if it puts you or someone else in a bad light. Doing this establishes trust and shows people that the parish is in this together and that the pastor, parish staff, trustees, and pastoral councils are trustworthy. I have one pastor in particular who did this very well: he was upfront and honest with his staff and leadership groups when an issue bubbled up and would always tell us immediately what he knew about it, or what the diocese was or wasn't doing about something. Our pastoral staff often felt privy to information that was "hot off the press." That kind of honest communication went a long way in helping all of us trust him and know he was working hard to ensure the health and longevity of our parish life. I never doubted him or wondered if he was playing games with us, nor ever considered him part of the kind of negative clerical culture that can, at times, thrive while unknowingly choking out all other life around it.

Once a difficult change is underway, a parish community must find ways to honor the past and usher in the future. Brainstorm a list of what is important to the parish's way of life, things that make the parish community who they are whether or not they are twinned, clustered, or merged—things the parish wants to hold on to no matter what. Also take time to make a list of what gifts or possibilities the Spirit may be opening to them in the future. How might parish life be different, for the better, when communities are mingled? Like the mingling of the water and wine in the Eucharistic Prayer, each retains its properties, but something new is created in that one shared Cup.

When a parish is being merged, the best-case scenario is when a new building can be built on new ground so both parish communities give up their space and enter it newly together. There is no getting around the difficulty of one community having to close its doors to join another community that remains in its own space, especially when it's a smaller community entering into a larger parish community. There is a very real feeling of being swallowed up by the larger community. Those remaining in their building have their pew, their Mass time, and their usual way of doing things and relating to others in the community.

So how can the community that remains find real and radical ways to welcome and make room for another community that is joining them? Perhaps a new name is chosen for the new parish that is being born, new Mass times begin so everyone is forced to create a new routine (including where they park and where they sit), and new committees and leadership structures are born. Another way of radically welcoming another parish community to one's own is to invite significant items to be brought over from the parish closing its doors to replace some items in the existing parish: key items such as the crucifix, the tabernacle, the holy water font, the altar, the ambo, or the Stations of the Cross are radical signs of welcome and a commitment to the new reality of shared parish life.

The diocese might send the bishop or his delegate to preside at a final Mass before a parish closes. The parish that is closing its doors could have a display of items of historical or sentimental significance. Anything from a parish history book to a bingo card, a scrapbook, a chalice, or to a large soup pot could make the cut. These items can be placed on display in the new parish if being merged, or placed in a time capsule and sealed for a future generation to open and enjoy a century or more from now. For items of liturgical value that will be used in the new parish, these can be included in more elaborate liturgical procession to the new space.

Sexual Abuse

As I've met with and listened to victims of sexual abuse by clergy, many want healing and restorative justice within the Church. Many would appreciate a chance to meet with their bishop, face to face, or to participate in a conversation circle that would include the bishop, a counselor, and other survivors. Many simply want to be seen and heard and acknowledged. Perhaps a candlelight march to the cathedral, followed by a Mass of healing where they might be the ones to extend their hands in blessing or offer words of healing and forgiveness to the Church rather than hear them would be in order. The tables can, appropriately enough, be reversed.

Local communities of faith also need rituals of healing. Our parishioners are hurt, betrayed, and wounded by the failure of our leaders and the absolute lack of moral credibility our Church now has about any issue.

Morale is low, and certainly people have walked away over this scandal. To a non-Catholic looking in, I've often wondered how this Church I love must look as more stories continue to come to the surface, and the answer in my mind is always the same: not good.

Pastoral leaders might consider planning a healing series for the faithful. Perhaps the 2015 movie *Spotlight* can be shown, which won two Academy Awards including Best Picture, with a discussion following. In addition, the 2008 movie *Doubt* would produce fascinating discussions if a parish wanted to do a two-night exploration of cinema followed by conversation. Popcorn and movie treats should be provided of course! A third and final night of the series would involve participants sharing in small circles. Each group would be equipped with a facilitator to ensure members all share equally and that confidentiality is honored. Each person would be asked to share their thoughts and feelings to four to five questions about the sexual abuse crisis. Questions might include the following:

- How have your thoughts changed about the scandal since first learning about it?
- How have your feelings changed since first learning of the scandal?
- How has the sexual abuse scandal affected your faith life?
- What has been the hardest part of the sexual abuse scandal for you?
- How do you think the scandal has affected the Catholic Church?
- What do you believe the Church needs to do next?

After adequate sharing, the facilitators invite participants to write something they believe the Church leadership needs to hear from them—whether it be their grief or anger or frustration or deep disappointment, allowing at least ten minutes to freely write. Assure them that what they write will remain private. Instrumental music can be played softly in the background as the participants prayerfully work, and tissues should be available in the room. After the allotted time, a gong is rung and participants come forward and circle around a burning bowl. One at a time, participants are invited to step forward and burn their journaling, symbolically releasing any hold these emotions may have over them. After all have finished, the pastoral leader invites each person to silently pray to the Holy Spirit, asking for the grace to forgive the Church leadership for her betrayal of our sacred trust we have so willing given since we ourselves have been children.

CONCLUSION

The final petition of the Lord's Prayer offers a balm to the crisis and can be a source for reflection or a prayer for healing: "and lead us not into temptation but deliver us from evil." Deliver us from evil! When the presider responds to this prayer with the words of the embolism, the short prayer said after the Lord's Prayer, there are more words of healing offered, like aloe vera to our wounds:

> Deliver us, Lord, we pray, from every evil,
> graciously grant peace in our days,
> that, by the help of your mercy,
> we may be always free from sin
> and safe from all distress,
> as we await the blessed hope
> and the coming of our Savior, Jesus Christ.

May these words bring some measure of comfort to all who struggle and feel pain as they pray at Mass.

A prayer we might make for the People of God is that, whenever there are difficulties with the decisions of the Church, in ways big or small, God's faithfulness might be known. May the faithful remember that God has not and will not ever fail them.

> For we know that if our earthly dwelling, a tent, should be destroyed, we have a building from God, a dwelling not made with hands, eternal in heaven.
>
> —2 Corinthians 5:1

CONCLUSION

The Spirit of the Lord is upon me,
because he has anointed me
to bring glad tidings to the poor.
He has sent me to proclaim liberty to captives
and recovery of sight to the blind,
to let the oppressed go free,
and to proclaim a year acceptable to the Lord.

—Luke 4:18–19

A young girl asked for and was given her very first Bible as a gift. She ran upstairs and excitedly began to read one of the Gospel accounts in its entirety as her mother continued to work in another part of the house. After a while, she could hear her daughter sobbing. Alarmed, she quickly went to her and asked her what was wrong. The little girl looked up with tears in her eyes and wailed, "Oh, no, they killed him!" Her mom went to her, wrapped her arms around her and held her for a long while. After her daughter's body had calmed down and her breath had returned to normal, her mom simply kissed the top of her head and said, "Keep reading, sweetie" and walked away.

Keep reading. What beautiful advice for all of us who do the work of justice, who work day in and day out ministering to God's people, who strive to live the Paschal Mystery. Keep reading. That is our call. As Easter people, amidst the suffering and tragedy, amidst the injustice and terror, amidst the absolutely inexplicable: we need only to keep reading. Somehow, someway, God is at work in the situation in which we find ourselves. Somehow, someway, light will be drawn forth from whatever terrifying darkness surrounds us. God always finds a way to draw straight from crooked lines. Life comes forth from the cold, dark tomb. The impossible is made possible. Tables are turned, God's ways are not our own, and God always acts in ways that are surprising. We need only to keep reading.

So preach these issues from the pulpit, write about them in the bulletin. Pick music that highlights our call to justice. Prepare prayer services that respond to immediate needs. Be hospitable and gracious. Add petitions regularly in the Universal Prayer. Connect the dots between Eucharist received and Eucharist lived. Gather the people for prayer, for action, for ritual, for conversation, and for healing in times of crisis or injustice. As pastors, deacons, ministers, and lay leaders, make the connection between what the faithful hear and see and struggle with every day in their lives and their faith. Silence can be deafening. I know. I've been in parishes where nobody is saying anything. So connect the dots. Ask yourself, and your community, what the Catholic response to a particular issue is. Grapple with it together. Our faith tradition has a lot to say about the issues of the day. It is not divisive, or too political, or controversial to do so. It is, rather, what our faith requires of us. Stand proudly on the firm ground of a century or more of Catholic social thought. We have nothing to lose and everything to gain as we hold this teaching to the light of the day.

As the Second Vatican Council sought to read the signs of the times. So must we. In the opening words of the *Pastoral Constitution on the Church in the Modern World*:

> The joys and hopes, the grief and anguish of the people of our time, especially of those who are poor or afflicted, are the joys and hopes, the grief and anguish of the followers of Christ as well. Nothing that is genuinely human fails to find an echo in their hearts. (1)

At my parish, we are offering a series of reflections by leadership titled "Why I Stay in the Church." The columns run in the weekend bulletin and are timely, personal pieces offered to the faithful at a time when it is not easy to remain Catholic. Our writers are offering pieces of their own faith story, with a willingness to be both honest and vulnerable as they share their own doubts and questions with the community. My colleague at the Basilica of St. Mary in Minneapolis, Johan van Parys, director of liturgy and sacred arts, reflected about the power of the Gospel, his love of the liturgy, his need for the Eucharist, and the way the faith community has sustained him during challenging personal times when he answered why he stays in the Church. This is how he reflected about his love for the Gospel:

> I stay because of my love for the Gospel. The Gospel truly is my guide and rudder on my journey. All of us carry our share of pain and suffering. And our world as a whole is in great agony. There are wars, civil unrest, natural disasters, disease, hunger, loneliness. Left to our own devices we are clearly unable to escape this spiral of death. The Gospel, when interpreted correctly, is an absolute antidote to all the evil that seems to control our world today. The Gospel is a most effective guide in our struggle to save humanity and all of creation. Such is the power of the Gospel.

The Gospel is, quite literally, the Good News of Jesus Christ. By looking back at the stories of our ancestors, of those first believers who also knew persecution, famine, war, drought, and injustice, it gives us hope. By looking backward, the Gospel alone has the uncanny ability to point us forward.

So our primary task as the Christian faithful in challenging times? Keep reading.

—Wendy Cichanksi Caduff

APPENDIX

Outline for Morning and Evening Prayer

Introductory Verse: *O God, come to my assistance. . . .*

Opening Hymn

Psalmody
> *One or two psalms plus a New Testament canticle (follows the first psalm at Morning Prayer; follows the second psalm at Evening Prayer)*

Reading *Short or longer reading from Scripture*

Homily or Reflection

Responsory

Canticle of Zechariah (morning) or Mary (evening)

The Lord's Prayer

Concluding Prayer

Blessing

Dismissal

Outline of Night Prayer

Examination of Conscience

Hymn

Psalmody *One or two psalms*

Reading *Short or longer reading from Scripture*

Responsory

Canticle of Simeon

Concluding Prayer

Blessing

Marian Antiphon *(such as the Salve Regina or Regina caeli)*

OUTLINE OF A SERVICE OF THE WORD

Opening Hymn
Sign of the Cross
Greeting
Opening Prayer
Readings
  Old Testament reading, Psalm, Gospel Acclamation, and Gospel
Homily or Reflection
[Optional Song/Words of Remembrance]
Intercessions
Lord's Prayer
Closing Prayer
Final Blessing
Dismissal
Closing Song

REFLECTION ON THE PRAYER SERVICES

We need to find ways to provide a space for people to reflect upon their encounters with the sacred through the words, gestures, songs, and movements of their prayer together—whether through Mass, a prayer service, or the Liturgy of the Hours. This might take place immediately after the experience or perhaps later in living rooms and around kitchen tables. Here are a couple of suggested discussion starters that can be used for most liturgical and paraliturgical experiences:

- What from the experience of praying together lingers for you? A song or scriptural image or story? Some words of reflection or a prayer text? A gesture or element in the worship space? Something else?

- What did you find meaningful or helpful about what you named? Or what new insights into [acts against human dignity] came about for you?